A Beautiful Choice

A Beautiful Choice

HOW TO GUIDE YOUR CHILD THROUGH LIFE-THREATENING ILLNESS, SUCCEED AND UNITE WITH YOUR CHILD

Gabriela Pattison

Rev. date: 05/10/2016

To order additional copies of this book, contact:
Xlibris
1-888-795-4274
www.Xlibris.com
Orders@Xlibris.com
711226

Contents

I would love to dedicate this book to the most inspiring people in my life!

Their unconditional love, compassion, and patience has been the driving force behind me becoming the person I am today!

Their forgiveness, as I stumbled along the way, has been the encouragement I needed to never give up!

The pureness of their hearts has been my strength to walk through the most challenging moments in my life with my head held high, looking toward the light instead of the darkness!

I love you, Jojo and Matthew!

It is not the adversity, challenge, or setback
that changes our lives!
It is in our journey to recognition that we always have
a beautiful choice we change!
That is where we grow, gain wisdom,
and find our true selves!
—Gabi Pattison

Acknowledgments

I would like to say thank you to my family and friends for standing by me on this journey and giving me the space I needed (and I needed a lot of space) to rediscover myself and life. I greatly appreciate the patience and support you have given me as I have been searching for true success in life. Because of your sacrifices, this book is not only a dream, but a real thing, and I know it wouldn't be possible without you guys. So I would like you to know how much everything you have done means to me and how grateful I am you are part of my life.

Thank you!

I would also like to say thank you to all the medical professionals that have worked hard on saving my son's life, keeping him smiling and comfortable as much as possible. I am very grateful for their commitment to get up every day and make it a day that is devoted to my child and millions of others. The kindness of their hearts, their knowledge, and their determination to keep going and never give up is a true inspiration.

Thank you!

Introduction

Does anything in life get you ready for a cancer of your child?
Is there a school, knowledge, logic,
or a piece of research that tells you how?

It is a dark, quiet night. I am sitting on the couch unable to do anything. No move, TV, word, or action. All I could think about is the answer to these questions. Jojo is seven years old, and Matthew is only three and a half years old. Cancer was never the word I thought would be in the same sentence as my son's name, but here I am. Now when I say his name, acute lymphoblastic leukemia, also known as ALL, follows his name. I have said the word *cancer* (in my head) millions of times since he has been diagnosed a couple of days ago, yet it does not feel real or going away. I have seen pediatric oncology (being a former nurse), and I have studied psychology, terms, and techniques on how to deal with traumatic situations, yet nothing has gotten me ready for the feeling I am feeling right now. I have never experienced such an excruciating pain. Nothing in life ever got me ready for this. Maybe that is why I have never searched for the diagnosis before the doctors said it out loud. I guess deep down I have known it is about more than any research, any knowledge, or any logical thinking. At least that is what I am feeling right now! The gut inside me is telling me I am not far from the truth.

It has taken me months to find the courage to trust my instinct and truly believe that little voice inside myself. I have read a lot of spiritual and motivational books, since I have known the answer isn't in the knowing. I am offering you my outlook in this book in the hope of saving you a lot of frustrations, misunderstandings, and confusion. We all have what it takes inside us to find our answer. All we need is just a little guidance, something to help us trust ourselves and recognize what we once knew but forgot. That is what *A Beautiful Choice* is all about—providing guidance and teaching you to recognize the state you are in, consequently producing the results you want.

All human behavior is the result of the state we are in.
—Anthony Robbins

It is so true yet easier said than done. The problem I was facing is that I thought I was in a different state than I actually was. I did everything the way I knew how, yet I wasn't getting the results I was expecting. Why weren't my actions aligning with my results? I have spent half of my life searching for the answer. I ascertained that I didn't have the right information. I always knew how we were taught as children plays a big part on how we live as adults and on the decisions we make. What I couldn't figure out for the longest time were the invisible influences behind everything we do.

Parenting is the most important job we can do and the most puzzling. Through generations, we learn techniques and habits on how to raise children without fully understanding what is behind the technique or habit. What each generation thinks is, we are going to make it work better. A few years into our parenting experience, we realize it is not working as we thought it would for us. We start struggling and searching for something better. Most of the time, we are not successful, because we don't see the influences. How could we? How can we see or understand something we have never been taught? It is really hard. For years I have studied parenting and how to be a better parent. I did improve, yet I felt there was more. I so desperately wanted to find the answer. I kept asking and searching until I got my answer. I just wasn't expecting it to show up like this.

On June 15, 2011, my three-and-a-half-year-old son, Matthew, got diagnosed with leukemia. Everything changed. I felt like everything I knew about anything was gone. I was standing in front of a blank white canvas ready to make my first stroke only to realize I was terrified to even pick up the brush. How do I draw a painting not having any clue about how to start or paint, along with the pressure of my baby's life depending on every stroke? I went into silence and isolation. Somehow I knew that was the best thing, and that is where I would find guidance and deeper understanding, along with answers of how parenting really works.

I started by grasping the fact that how we feel, what energy we carry, and how much pain we hold in our hearts has more influence in parenting than any technique or habit. It took me years to see that parenting is everything I thought it isn't. That is when I discovered the seven influences that play a major part in our parenting as well as our everyday lives, whether we want to or not. They are the roots to successful being, parenting, as well as getting the results we want based on understanding the state we are in. They provide answers to how to parent a child through life-threatening illness, succeed, and unite with our children.

Therefore, my brush strokes started to fill the canvas with a painting of a truly beautiful tree. With each stroke, I got stronger, my roots grew deeper, and my understanding and healing started to produce the results I have always hoped for but never got. It was challenging, lonely, and a lot of times felt like invisible work, but I knew if I stayed consistent and persistent, it would pay off. It took a long time, just like it takes years to grow a healthy, strong tree that is able to withstand any storm, but at the end, it has been all worth it. Taking the time with each stroke to nurture the roots and trunk (understanding the influences and healing) helped grow a prolific tree that gave out all the ripe fruit (results I wanted).

The title, *A Beautiful Choice*, was born in a writers club I was part of. We would share part of our work with each other and provided feedback for one another. I shared part of the first chapter about our day before diagnosis. As I was listening to my first feedback, I heard "what a beautiful choice" comment about our exploring trip to find the hospital. In that instant, I knew it was the perfect title for the book, because it flawlessly describes the message of this book.

A Beautiful Choice is about creating a space that will allow us to have a moment of recognition so we can make an appropriate choice that will produce the results we want. It is about learning how to find ourselves within, get more comfortable about operating from a place of love, and become skilled at how to guide and empower all the abilities that we and our children already have within.

Most of all, it is about changing the biggest misunderstanding in parenting, especially when facing one of the toughest challenges. Which is, parents have to be strong, flawless, perfect, know everything, and do everything in order to be *good* parents. We could not have been farther from the truth. What do I mean by that? The minute it was confirmed that Matthew had acute lymphoblastic leukemia (ALL) was the same moment I acknowledged (quietly inside) I had no idea how to face this challenge.

In our family, hard times or scary situations were not really handled well, and they weren't talked about. I think it was first to protect us children from bad things in life and also in the hope that if we don't dwell in the condition, it would work itself out without anybody noticing the bad and the hard life has to offer. It was also partially because my parents weren't taught how to deal with fear and scary moments. That is also the reason I went into silence. I couldn't prove it then, but I knew if I was going to pretend to be someone I was not at that moment (stronger, better), it would only create anger, frustration, and resentment. Trying to be stronger than I was, more knowledgeable, or look like I could do it all would only make my kids feel like they were not good enough, like they were less than. *Why? Because the "perfect parent" (strong, flawless, and know-and-do-it-all) is constantly in a fearful state of mind, and fear always makes people around us feel less than.*

This is one of the misunderstandings and, I believe, the biggest in parenting. *We were taught to believe that always being in control, strong, and brave and having answers to anything meant we were acting out of love, but opposite is the truth.* Fear is behind our every thought or action. That is also why we have not been getting the results we want.

The loving parent is imperfect, vulnerable, scared, open-minded, a good listener, and hardly ever strong or put together. All these have to come out loud in our words and actions as we guide our children through life, especially when they are facing life-threatening illness, or being a sibling to a child with one.

The moment we admit our imperfections and fears, along with daring to be vulnerable to our children, is the instant they feel loved, empowered, embraced, honored, and good enough, and same goes for the inner child inside all of us. What we give to ourselves we are able to give to our children! So to get the results we want, we have to get ourselves to the loving state of mind. The minute I did (don't get me wrong, it was not always easy), parenting became breathtakingly beautiful as well as empowering, and I got the results I have always strived for.

What I would like all parents to get from this book is that no matter what challenges life brings our way, we always have an opportunity to chose, even if it doesn't seem that way in the moment, just by recognizing the state we think and act out of. That is what *A Beautiful Choice* is about.

Empowerment!

Instinct

What if I already know what to do?

It is a nice warm morning, June 14, 2011. I woke up early to have a cup of coffee, read my book, and have my mommy time before the day begins like I usually do. I know this day is going to be very different. I have known for months, but today is the day it is going to come out. Today is the day to face the biggest fear any parent can face.

My munchkins are going to be getting up soon, so let me go over the schedule for the day real quick. Deep breath. I run through the day in my head, feeling very overwhelmed. We have an appointment with the kids' dentist at 10:00 a.m. and an appointment with our pediatrician at 4:45 p.m. Matthew needs to have a nap in the middle of the day (because he has been very tired lately). I have to get lunch and dinner ready because I won't have time to cook after the doctor's appointment. Will there be enough time for everything? The dentist is only a two minutes drive, and we shouldn't be there longer than an hour; it is just a cleaning. It will give us enough time to have lunch at 12:00 p.m. and nap right after. A snack right after Matt gets up, whenever that will be, get dressed, and leave for the checkup. Drive time to our pediatrician's office is about thirty minutes each way, so we should be home by 6:30 p.m. for dinner. We won't have time for swimming today, but it's OK; we can swim all day tomorrow. OK, there is enough time for everything. Good.

I stay sitting in my comfy chair with a cup of coffee, and my book, which at this point doesn't have any of my attention, and a blank stare. I feel all these emotions moving through my body—my heart is racing, and the fear is taking over. My thoughts are all over the place. I know something is really wrong, but I haven't been ready to face the reality of the situation (I don't think as a parent you ever are). I am imagining all the scenarios in my head (of course the denial version). What could the doctor say? Why is Matt so tired all the time? Why does the bronchitis keep coming back? Why is he yellow looking? Why is his heart beating so fast? Why is he in so much pain? I hope he is going to get up this morning. I am so scared. With all honesty, I can't come up with any answers. Right after I ask the questions, my brain goes blank. No assumptions, no diagnosis of any kind, nothing. Just nothing. All I know is that something is really wrong. My pain is so unbearable that my brain can't even think straight. In today's world of Internet and information I can probably find the answer, but I don't want to. Not yet anyway. I stay sitting in my chair for a while, like I have been every morning for the last couple of months, just knowing something is wrong but not having the courage to go and search. I guess deep down I know, I will find out at the right time. I just want a little more time to get ready. I want to know how to get ready.

The sound of my babies' voices waking up all happy and laughing snap me out of my numbness. It is the nicest sound, followed by a sense of relief. After greeting them with hug, kiss, and smile, it is time to get ready for the day. First, breakfast and then our dental appointment. Jojo and Matthew are going to have so much fun; they love the dentist's office. They ride the chair up and down, get tickled by the funny toothbrush, and of course get a present to go home with.

As we sit at the dentist's office and talk, they notice Matthew's slightly yellow color. I am sitting and hoping maybe they (staff) will say it is something little and it will become true, but at the same time, I'm saying to myself, they are dentists, not pediatricians. I know better, but I still hope. We finish our appointment and head back home.

I am making the kids lunch, secretly hoping I am dreaming and will wake up soon. After the kids eat, Matthew is going to take a nap. I am trying to relax but can't. All of a sudden, the time starts to move fast, or so it seems. Matt is up now, so we are eating a snack then get in the car to leave for the doctor's appointment. All I am thinking is, thank you, God, for keeping Matthew alive and safe for now. I am wishing I could freeze the time but, at the same time, knowing it wouldn't help anything.

We are at the doctor's office. It starts out as a regular visit; he is checking the ears, nose, and lungs. Then he asks Matt to lie down, and he is feeling Matt's belly. I am staring at the doctor's face as he is examining Matthew, watching his expressions, trying to see his reaction. All of a sudden, I see it, the doctor's face is so serious yet so calm, because he knows I have to be able to drive to the hospital. I am looking at the kids to see if they are noticing anything.

I find the courage to ask the doctor, "What is it?"

Even though he knows, he says very calmly, "It's hard to tell without further tests, so why don't you take a drive to the Park Ridge Hospital emergency room sometime soon?"

And my first question is, "How soon are you talking?" (That shows how much I am not ready to hear it, and at that point, I am in shock).

Again he said very calmly and casually, "If you want to stop home to pack some clothes, that's fine, but tonight or tomorrow the latest would be best."

Clothes for what? Thankfully, all these conversations are in my head, because I don't want to say or ask anything that could scare the kids or even raise any suspicion.

I feel numbness and tingling all over my body. I know this is it! We are going to find out! I am just praying to God not to take Matt away. I am saying as calmly as I can, "OK"—but my voice is shaking, and I just want to fall down on my knees, fall apart, and cry—"what is the address, and how do we get there?" Inside, I am talking to myself, *Focus, pay attention, you have to find that hospital,* but it is so hard. I can see the doctor talking but feel myself disappearing far away. Nothing is making sense; it is like he isn't even speaking the same language. Finally, I am able to snap back, because I feel the kids are watching. I numb everything I am feeling, get myself together (at least on the surface), and am able to make sense of the directions.

"Let me call their dad to let him know what is happening, get the kids ready, and announce to them 'we are going on an exploring adventure.'" This is also my first moment realizing that any moment can take our breath away. Right now my heart is filled with overwhelming amount of gratitude for this split second. I feel like it is a never ending moment while holding on to the feeling of it, because I have no idea if I will get many more moments with Matthew. The exploring adventure trip is a fun ride despite all the fear and panic, because I feel so present for the ride and I am not thinking about the near future. *Every trice, every split second of our lives counts, even if nobody else sees it or knows about it. All that matters is how we feel as we go through each moment we are given along with how we make people around us feel!* "The doctor said we have to find this hospital, and we have never been this way, so you guys can help Mommy find it, right?" They are a little confused, but they are going along with my game of exploring.

We say bye to the ladies at the front desk and leave. All I am thinking is *How can I make this fun?* or should I say, *How do I cover the situation up so the kids don't have a clue, knowing very well they know?* Kids pick up on parents' energies better than parents do on their own sometimes. They sense something is wrong, especially Matthew, because he knows how he has been feeling the last couple of months. He might not have words, but kids are incredibly intuitive, more than we give them credit for. The incredible little human beings my kids are, they are going with it. We get into our car and start heading for the hospital, wherever that is. To make it more fun, I announce we are stopping at McDonald's for dinner. They are screaming with excitement, "Yeee, this is going to be fun exploring!" (Eating out is a very special treat for us; it only happens on special occasion.) They are asking questions like, "How do we find the hospital?" "What clues should we look for?" "How long will it take?" "Do you have the directions?" They are so cute and thinking so clearly. All I can do right now is ask God to guide me. I have nothing; all I know is that I don't know *how.*

One dinner, laughs, and fun exploration later we find the hospital. We walk into the emergency room. I give them the paperwork from our pediatrician. They go through the routine admission, and all of a sudden, we are following them to the room. All I am thinking is, *How long is this going to take?* It's after dinner, about six-thirty-ish. Matt had a nap, but he has been so tired lately. We need to be back by nine so he can get his rest. "What about the bill?" From the seriousness of the doctor's face, it will probably be really high, because they have to do all these tests. And as I am thinking this, I am saying to myself, *Are you crazy?* None of this matters. Your life is about to change big. I guess in a way I am still hoping life will be back to normal after the visit, that it will be an infection or something; we will get antibiotics and go home.

A few tests and hours later and we still don't have a straight answer. They are saying something about his white blood cells count, maybe infection, and they have to run more tests (they know they just can't say it without the bone-marrow test to make it real). I am still hopeful or trying to deny the real situation at this point, thinking: *Rare infection–that's not that bad. We are in America and have modern medicine. They have a cure,* but I am not feeling what I am thinking.

They come back and say we will have to get admitted to the hospital because Matthew needs two transfusions tonight. "Hold it right there. Transfusion for what? If you don't know what it really is, why does he need transfusion? *I am thinking what if the blood is infected with HIV virus and he gets sick?*" Nothing is making sense. I look at the kids to see if they are scared, and I see they are. They don't want to show it or say much, but I can feel it. I can see on their faces they have all these questions that I don't know how to answer yet, and they don't know how to ask. I don't want to scare them for no reason. I can feel the panic in the room, or maybe it is just me?

I know Jojo is crying because she has to go home with Dad and she can't be there for Matthew (they have never been apart). I am telling her that "It's OK. Mommy will take care of Matthew. You will come in the morning to visit." Somehow we all manage to calm down a little.

While later, because it still isn't making sense to me, I step outside to find the ER doctor to ask some question to make at least a little sense of things. I am really trying to understand, but I can't.

Finally, the doctor looks at me and says, "We have a suspicion for leukemia but can't say for sure till we do further tests."

I am so glad I am outside and the kids can't see me because I feel my body breaking down. Tears are flooding my face, my body falling down to my knees (even though I am standing), I feel like vomiting, and I am looking at the doctor with the numb stare in my face. It is my first out-of-body experience. As painful as this moment feels, there is something magical in it if you think about it. I don't have to do anything, just *be*, and my body takes care of all the necessary actions to protect itself. I keep looking at the doctor hoping she will say it's not true, but she is not. I don't know how I got to the bathroom, but here I am, standing in the bathroom just crying. I want to think, but I can't. Luckily, the doctor followed me and is trying to talk to me to calm me down. She is saying something that I know I will never forget and I feel that it is going to be one of our biggest life-changing clues in the journey. She is holding my face up, looking into my eyes—she wants to make sure I hear her—and saying, "If your child is to get anything [any bad disease], you want it to be leukemia, because today's treatment is so advanced." Even though I want to say, "What are you talking about? I don't want my child to have anything," I am listening. After a second, I hear what she is really saying.

That moment changed my life forever because she has given me the power of choice, *a beautiful choice* (another breathtaking moment), to take the big *C* out of cancer through opening my eyes to the possibility of having the power of choice to make this an amazing and unforgettable time of our life instead of the most miserable. I know it's not going to be an easy one, but it's going to be life changing for our whole family. We will not be surviving every day; we will be living every day like we never did before. *There are moments in our lives that no matter how bad things get, when we really listen, we get the answer or guidance right in the midst of all the rain. All we have to do is to have the courage to listen.*

The conversation is over, and I am able to go back to the room, and even though I am still processing the information, I am able to observe myself and all my feelings on the inside instead of lashing them in fear and anger on the outside. I am able to answer the kids' questions to the best of my knowledge without scaring them. I am able to comfort them in the hardest time of our life, and that is a breathtaking moment for me, because I have never thought I could. In this moment, in this room, I feel the power of *a beautiful choice* again, and it is the most amazing feeling. I am not saying that we aren't scared—of course all of us are—but we are there for each other. We are so present in this moment, because our fear is so big we don't know what is going to happen in the future.

After we all start to feel somewhat comforted (*safe* would be another word I will use a lot, because our life's biggest obstacle is feeling safe, and if we don't, it triggers fear and anger), we are transported from the emergency room to the children's floor in the hospital. Jojo knows she can't stay but is asking if she can walk upstairs with us because she would feel more comfortable (safe), knowing where her brother is going, before she goes home. So we all are heading upstairs to check out the room.

Right before leaving the ER, I am feeling inkling sensation taking over me to let me know I need to pay attention. I feel this is going to be the most important night of my life, providing me with guidance and answers to *how*. I am looking around the ER with a sense of presence and peace, looking to see what I am supposed to see, trying to understand what I am supposed to understand, saying thank you to God (in my head) while turning around to step ahead toward our new life filled with the unknown.

We are making the best of riding a bed (coolest thing ever) for the first time in their short life, something I never thought they will have to experience. Now that it is here, we are making the most fun out of it and are enjoying it. When life gives you lemons, make lemonade, right?

We are in our room now. My friend is on her way; she's coming shortly. I give Jojo kisses and tell her that I will take good care of her brother and she will come visit in the morning. I so want to promise her he will be OK, but can't. The way I am feeling right now, so unsure of anything (including if he is going to be OK), I can't make a promise I might not be able to keep. Never did, never will. *We should only make promises we can keep to build trust in all relationships; therefore, it is one of the most crucial factors of this journey.*

My friend is staying for a while, she says as long as I need, and I am feeling very grateful and will never forget how amazing and supportive she is being. We are in the bathroom again (I never realized how therapeutic bathrooms can be) because I am feeling my body falling apart for the second time tonight (it comes in waves, I guess). I can't really comprehend what she is saying, but it feels comforting. I think her being here, her presence, is more than the words. Coming out of the bathroom, I am able to face more challenges the night will have to offer, at least for a while till I feel like falling apart again.

I kiss Jojo and Allynn and say good night so they can go home. After they leave, we are sitting on the couch with my friend in our new room. Right before my friend is about to leave, she asks me, "Do you have socks?"

"It is hot outside, so I am just wearing sandals."

She takes off the socks she is wearing and says, "Here, keep these. Do you know how cold it gets in the hospital?"

I don't know how cold it gets in the hospital, but what I know is that it is one of the sweetest things somebody has ever done for me. I don't know if I am crying on the outside (I am not good at showing emotions), but I am definitely crying on the inside. It is one of those moments that will stay with me forever. At the same time, I know that even though it is going to be the hardest thing I will have to go through in life, there is always going to be support if I choose to see it.

My friend leaves. It is the first time I am alone with my baby and our new life. I crawl in bed with him and we cuddle (or as we say muddle-cuddle with Mommy). The room is quiet; it is almost midnight, but at this moment for the first time all night, the fear is gone. We feel safe and peaceful. We have each other to hold on to, and nothing else matters. For a little while, we lie snug together without words, just listening to each other's heartbeats and just being in the moment, being happy to be able to be together. It is a breathtakingly unforgettable moment because of how present we are. We don't know what tomorrow is going to bring, but we know right now we are together and happy even if just for a little while.

Matthew is sleeping. I am sitting on the couch, watching him sleep and my life is flashing in front of me. I call Allynn (my then husband) to see if he made it home safe with my princess. He says they did and that she is sleeping. There isn't much conversation because neither of us knows what to really say. We say good night and hang up. I keep sitting on the couch staring out the window to try to make a plan; instead, thoughts are flying through my head in unorganized order, yet somehow they are making sense. Somehow I feel that I will know what to do every step of the way. I just will not know the whole plan now. I stay sitting there most of the night, and for the first time ever, this is the longest I am able to be present in the moment. *The fear of what tomorrow going to bring is giving me the freedom of just being.* I have heard of freedom before, yet never really felt it like this night.

The night went by fast. The sun is starting to rise and the room is filling with daylight. Holding a fresh cup of coffee, I am watching Matt, so breathtakingly handsome three-and-a-half-year-old little boy that has my heart filled with so much love, trying to take it all in. Even though it is one of the hardest night of my life, at the same time, it is the most peaceful and life changing. Anything that is going to follow after this night is going to be so fully lived. I feel it. And that is my greatest gift. I know it, just can't put it in words. *Freedom comes from living every moment in our life through our true selves, not our ego, whether good or bad, sad or happy. As humans, we are given the privilege of experiences and we miss so much of it by setting up the rules about how, when, or what we should experience. By being present, we allow ourselves to let the moments flow through our bodies and learn exactly what we need at any given moment.*

My pumpkin is starting to open his eyes. I smile and greet him to a new day with an affirmation that I am here and we are safe for now. Today is the day we are going to find out. Doctors and nurses start to come to the room to get Matt ready for the bone-marrow test. Everything is happening so fast. New information keeps coming in faster than we can remember it, let alone process it.

It is time to transport Matt to ICU. Even though it is a short walk, we are practically next door, it is the most challenging one.

I am feeling anything and everything, from sadness, fear, anger, hopelessness to hope (it might not be cancer), love, and gratefulness for having this moment. No matter what is happening, we are together. At the same time, I am sad I can't be with my baby girl (mother's guilt, no matter how much I do, I feel like I should do more), but being pushed to the corner like this, I know I can only be with one of my babies. I have two choices: (1) feel guilty and focus on what I am not doing or (2) be present and focus on what I am doing. I feel guidance telling me if I choose the first option, I won't be able to be there for anyone. Guilt will take away from my presence, which means I can't really be there for Matthew, and he really needs me now, which would make me feel even worse about me, and that would create more pain, which would make me incapable of being there for Jojo when I see her.

We make it to the ICU. The room starts to fill up with doctors, nurses, anesthesiologists, and people that are going to assist with the procedure. I am feeling so overwhelmed and scared. I know that this procedure is going to be it. This is going to be the answer to our new life and there is no turning back. There is no more "Hold on" and "I am not ready." Right now is the moment of "Ready or not, here it come."

The procedure is anything but smooth. First, the anesthesia isn't working, then Matt rips out the IV, and the doctor handling that part of the procedure has a really bad energy. Out of nowhere, I hear myself asking the doctor to fix her energy or leave the room. It surprises me, hearing myself say that to an authority and someone who is dealing with my son's life, but the love for my baby is stronger than the fear of judgment. She asks me if she needs to leave the room. "No" I said, "you just have to fix your energy, because what you are doing is not working. I am sure you are an excellent doctor. It's just at this moment, your energy is getting in the way of doing your job." I don't know how, but she did it. I can feel the shift in energies as it is happening. With great difficulties, the doctor is able to get enough bone marrow. The moment of truth is in the little cup.

The procedure is over and we are able to return back to our room. I feel relief. There is that moment again, that breathtaking moment of just being. We are exhausted and scared from the procedure, and it has left us speechless and present. It is easier to be in the present moment than to be in the future. Even if the future is a couple of hours from now or a couple of days. This is the first time I have realized the power of a present moment.

Another night is here, Matt falls asleep, and I am sitting on the couch quietly looking out the window, like the other night, thinking about the day. I keep replaying the moment of anesthesia and my comment to the doctor about her energy. I have a feeling that energy is going to play a big part in our journey, just can't quite get how. Despite my fear of judgment, I put up a sign on the door that says,

Please pay attention to the energy you bring into this room.

—**B. Taylor**

I don't really understand it and definitely can't put it in words, but it feels good. I know I need to remember the feeling of this moment.

Another morning is here faster than I am ready for it. We have the diagnosis, acute lymphoblastic leukemia. So I guess after all, we got what we should have wished for, as the doctor in the ER said. Confusingly, I am feeling relief that it is just leukemia, thanks to the ER doctor. Don't get me wrong, I am scared too, but somehow the feeling that it is just leukemia makes more sense to hang on to than to hang on to the feeling of "it is *cancer*" (fear and pain).

The next couple of days are going to get busy. The doctors want to start the chemotherapy as soon as possible. We are scheduling Matthew's surgery to put his medi port in for the next day, so they can start chemo treatment on Friday. Medi port is a little device that the doctors implant underneath his skin so they can draw blood and give chemotherapy without having to poke his arms every time he gets treatment.

Days are taking on a whole new speed. It is yet another morning and the day of Matthew's surgery. We are getting ready to take another fun ride in the bed. Transport is here, and courageously or not, we are heading for a new life filled with surgeries, procedures, treatments, chemo, and who knows what else. I am looking at Matthew's face while walking. It is filled with joy and fun on one side from riding in the bed, but fear, hesitation, and wonder on the other side about the unknown of what is about to happen. We are in the preoperational room. My best friend is here with us as well as Nanny (my close friend's mom) and I am trying to hold it together. Surgeries scare me and looking at my little baby boy—so innocent, fragile—makes me feel so helpless.

"Time to go," says the surgeon.

I kiss my baby boy, telling him how much I love him, slowly letting go of his hand as he gets further and further away, while holding back my tears and the feeling of wanting to die because of how hopeless I am feeling right now. At the same time, I am realizing that I will never be able to protect him and that it is not my job as parent to do so. *The only way to be a good parent is by providing guidance for our children and for what life brings their way.* My question is, how am I supposed to do that?

Matthew is still in surgery while the oncologist comes to talk to me. I am so grateful to have my best friend sitting next to me. She is an amazing friend. I called her the night we got admitted to the hospital. I would never, in a million years, expect her to do what she did. She put her life on hold in a second to come and be here for me. She left her husband and two kids and flew in from Washington, D.C. the next day. I am and will forever be grateful to her and her husband, because Allynn had to be home with our princess (at scary times like this, there is nothing better for a little girl than to have her daddy next to her).

As we are sitting in the little room and the doctor is trying to explain once again what is going on, I feel myself floating away from my body. I look at my friend with the feeling of "Please help me [don't actually say the words]. Catch me and bring me back to my body." As I start to feel like I am going to pass out, somebody makes a loud noise in the hallway. I think the doctor is sensing I need a moment, so he stops talking to pay attention to the hallway noise. I am grateful for that noise. It is giving me a chance to return to my body and gain enough clarity to finish the conversation. I am not comprehending much of it, but I am able to finish it. "Any questions?" he asks. I am asking questions I am not sure I want to know answers to, but again I am still not ready for any of this either. Getting the answers, which I am still not sure what they really mean, we are able to say our goodbyes and return to the waiting room.

We are sitting in the waiting room with my best friend for a little while after the conversation, trying to make sense of anything that has been said. Thankfully, they are calling me into post–operating room to go see Matthew. I really don't want to be thinking about something I have absolutely no idea about. All I want is to be with my baby boy. Seeing my baby lying in the bed is one of my most challenging times. I am so happy to see he is alive, yet the feeling of fear, sadness, pain, and exhaustion takes over my body without my permission, knowing this is just the beginning of something much bigger and more exhausting. Right now I am feeling like I can't take anymore two days into the news. How am I going to do it for three more years? Being next to my baby, holding his hand, just being, is all I have.

Days are passing by and more challenging decisions are presented at us with each day. It has been a couple of days since we found out Matthew has cancer, yet this morning I am looking at his oncologist as he is asking me if we are going to go with standard treatment or if we would like to participate in clinical trial. *How can he be asking me that right now?* is the only thought passing through my brain. I'm not ready to answer that. I hear myself asking him to give us a couple of days to decide or maybe a week. He is really kind about it and says he can only give us a couple of days. I am feeling it's not enough time, but know deep down no matter how much time he would give us, it would never be enough.

Another night is here, more challenging than the one before. Matthew is asleep as I am sitting very quietly on the couch, hoping that the right answer will come to me. Hours of silence are passing by and I am starting to feel the answer. *Give up control of knowing what's going to be tomorrow. Choose presence of love over fear of tomorrow.* So as scared as I am of surrendering my control over the future, I know the answer that is coming from the loving part of me is to go with the clinical study. It is a scary decision, but I feel it is coming out of loving place and not fear; therefore, we are going to be OK. I am choosing to do the clinical study, because of all the families that made the same decision like me, my son has a chance to live today and in the future. Because those families said yes out of love versus no out of fear, the research for cure in childhood cancer is where it is today.

Sunlight is filling the room again and I am looking at my baby boy opening his beautiful blue eyes. It is affirming my decision. We have breakfast in bed together, and with my cup of coffee, I am signing the papers for clinical study. With that signature, I am surrendering any control over what the future is going to bring. It is the scariest yet the most liberating moment of my life. Overcoming that fear is giving me a sense of freedom to live my life based on choices and decisions that come out of love instead of fear. I have never felt so proud and sure of anything in my life like I am feeling of this right now. Along with handing the paperwork to the doctor, I handed him the life as I knew it, creating a better one for all of us.

I am handing him the paperwork and he hands me back yet another fact. Three years and four months is the time it is going to take for my baby boy to go through the treatment. Hearing that news is way over the capacity of my brain to understand. I am trying, but at the same time, my brain is going blank. It is like trying to teach a two-year-old how to build a skyscraper. No matter how hard you try, the two-year-old is not going to get it. That's how I am feeling right now hearing the length of the treatment. I can hear my brain repeating *three years four months*, but no matter how many times I hear myself say it, it is not sinking in. At the same time, my need to know how it's going to end is coming to visit. New situation brings new challenges, and I am trying to surrender like I did with the clinical trial, just not successfully yet. Just tell me what's coming. I can deal with the end result (so I think). I just don't know how to deal with the process. At the same time as I am thinking that, I am answering to myself. The doctors don't know how it's going to end. They know how to treat leukemia, but they can't make any guarantees. It is another memorable moment for me. I am realizing there isn't a parent out there that knows how to deal with the process at the moment you find out the diagnosis. At the same time, I feel that cancer is about the process and not the end result. The blessing and liberating thing in this moment is my realization that I have control over absolutely nothing; it holds a certain sense of freedom. This journey is showing me that parenting is not about controlling my life and the life of my children; it's about living it. I have always thought that if I can control the situations in my kids' life, I can protect them. But at this moment, I am realizing that I am not able to protect them, but I can definitely enjoy them and everything they have to offer.

It is Friday morning, the day of our first chemotherapy. Life of unexpectedness is starting, or is it? Right now I have no hopes, expectations, dreams, plans, or fear. I am fully present, focusing on trying to catch each message that is passing by every second of every day trying to show me my way to true, unconditional love, free of unnecessary fear.

It has been a week. We are getting ready to go home for the first time since we found out Matthew has cancer. I am just starting to feel safe in the hospital, and now I have to go and face our new life outside of these few walls. I am not ready, but nobody is really asking or seems to be concerned about my readiness. I am on my own, at least that is how I am feeling right now. I wonder if Matthew feels the same way. All I can say out loud with a smile though is, are you ready to go home, pumpkin? Feeling scared, I am signing discharge papers unready and terrified to step into the direction of our whole new life, trying to remember that

Cancer is our guide to being, bringing us everything we long for if we choose to see it.

A Beautiful Choice is about providing you with the opportunity to see beyond the visible.

Summary

I have learned you have what you need within. Underneath your fear, doubt, and self-judgment, you have the power of knowing the next step that is the right one for you.
I discovered the seven invisible influences to help you walk through your journey the way you want and need.
The seven invisible influences are the following:

- **Instinct**—always go with that feeling no matter how uncertain it may seem.
- **Fear**—use it as a guidance to love and what you want, because fear will never fully disappear from your life.
- **Present moment**—don't miss this moment no matter how bad or good for something that might never come.
- **Ego**—recognize your thought from reality, and you can gain a clear, objective point of view of the situation.
- **Expectation**—sometimes not knowing is the greatest blessing. Watch your child set their expectations, and set your own. Don't let anybody else do it for you.
- **Listening**—this journey is all about feeling validated and acknowledged, not about knowing everything. You need to feel safe, and the only way to provide safety is through listening.
- **Education**—it is about learning to get to know your bodies and your bodies' response to challenging situations. It is about feelings and reaction to feelings and very little about the facts of the illness.

Fear

**What if cancer could be my second chance to be
the person and parent I have always wanted?**

The night is beautifully black. I am looking out the window watching
the flashing lights of cars go by, feeling like I am in a movie. It still
doesn't feel real. The last couple of days have been so surreal I am
trying to catch up on everything that has been said and that has
happened. I know there is a big lesson hiding in everything that is
happening. I can feel it; I know it is living life fully not based on fearful
decisions. What I am trying to figure out is, how am I supposed to
surrender fear in the scariest time of my life? I can feel how, but my
mind, or should I say ego, is trying to convince me otherwise. Trying
to prove I am right and my instinct is wrong. How am I going to do it?
How am I supposed to not be afraid when my son just got diagnosed
with leukemia? How do I surrender fear in the midst of the scariest
time of my life? Just thinking about it is scary.

In my family, we have never talked about scary things or
challenging times. When something bad happened, the whole family
got silent. I remember when my grandfather got diagnosed with
cancer, nobody said anything, at least not to us children, and we were
nineteen and twenty-two years old, so really, we were grown-ups. I
would go visit him at the hospital not having any clue that he had
cancer. When I asked the question why he was there, I would never

get a straight answer and knew not to ask again. I know they wanted to protect us as babies from the bad things that happen in life. I was grateful for it my whole life until or unless something bad happened to me and I didn't know how to deal with the situation. This is one of those moments, only this time, I can't run, avoid, or pretend it isn't happening. In the quiet hospital nights like this one, I am thinking, *If only my parents taught me how to handle the hard stuff in life. Would I be feeling differently right now? How am I supposed to handle such a huge thing when I can't even handle the little things?*

Then it dawns on me. Maybe they did teach me, at least how to start. Maybe by not talking about cancer based on feelings of fear and assumptions, or not giving cancer the big *C*, is exactly the way to handle this situation in our life, at least for now. I don't know if it is right, but feel it is the right start. The way I am explaining it to myself is like this, I will do it this way for now and adjust as we go.

Matthew is three and a half years old. Him not really understanding the disease is a blessing. It doesn't put any limitations on how he wants to live his life. We can learn together how to deal with each day and moment. We don't have to talk about the future a lot. At first, we did tell the kids the treatment will be three years and four months long, but it hasn't been imaginable for any of us. So we gave up the idea of the whole picture and are focusing on the little steps.

We are home now. I am learning how to live our new life outside of hospital walls and safety of doctors at the press of a button. I am so paralyzed by fear, the fear of what to say—so I don't put ideas to the kids' innocence that don't need to be there. By the fear of other people's opinions on how to handle this situation and their openness of talking about everything in front of the kids. By the fear of doctor's visits and what might be said there, that I am losing my voice and starting to withdraw from a lot of people and situations. I am so fragile and scared. I know I won't be able to explain or defend what I am doing. Maybe because I am not sure that what I am doing is the right thing. I know I want to keep the kids lives innocent as much as possible, but I am even doubting if that is the right thing. I am just going to go with my instinct, right or wrong I am listening to it.

We have not spent any time trying to logically understand cancer, control it, or put unnecessary fears in our life (I can't handle that, so I am using the denial stage for this step in our journey). *Cancer is not about gaining control over life, it is about surrendering it while opening our hearts to something bigger and better, LOVE.* Things are scary and overwhelming enough without controlling outcome. Instead, we are focusing on the emotional side of getting through checkups and procedures, only asking what we need to do until we come the next time. I can't ask what each medicine is for, how the body might react to it, or what the possible side effects are. I think because deep down, I know the more we know about it, the more we will live up to it, whether we realize it or not. Subconscious is a powerful thing.

It is frustrating at times because part of me (the fear part) wants to be able to control the cancer and its outcome. Thankfully though, I haven't really had the opportunity, and that really puts me in the place of surrender. I have had to let go of the certainty (at least for the most part) of how life is going to be. I am going from being sure how tomorrow, next week, or next year is going to be (so I thought) to not being certain of what the next hour is going to bring. On one side, it is the scariest feeling ever, but on the other side, it is so liberating.

As days and weeks go by, I am starting to search for a way to get fear out of my life because living in it or working on getting rid of it is so intense, so exhausting. This is the anger stage of grief for me. Even though I know I have what I need within, for the first time in my life—not that I am perfect; I feel complete though—I keep longing for people's approval and understanding of me and what I am experiencing. I want their compassion, understanding, and companionship. I am looking for someone to be in it with me. Someone to stand beside me, listening to me as I am saying and searching for my next move out loud, without judgment, disapproval, or making me feel that being different due to our challenge is making me unlovable. It is a hard crossroad for me. Choosing the path of love where I feel complete and at peace, yet by myself, as opposed to the fear path where everybody is, along with the hope that things are different than they really are yet feeling more lonely, is one of the greatest challenges on this journey. It has been taking me the longest time. Letting go of this fear path and choosing love has been my greatest accomplishment. Along with this crossroad, I am standing in front of another one pretty much at the same time.

How do I deal with such an intense feeling of unfailing fear? I only have so long before I will break down, and since that is not an option, I have to figure out a different plan. So far I have asked for guidance, and this situation isn't an exception. I am hoping for a quick fix. I am tired and overwhelmed. I can't handle another obstacle. I want the right-now and easy answer. As we all know, life doesn't work that way.

I am feeling my answer is starting to form. For a couple of weeks now it has been appearing in a different situation. I have been feeling it. It feels so right yet so wrong. I have been doubting the feeling. It feels so effortless yet so improper. I have acted in response to the feeling on occasion, and every time I did, it got me the result I wanted. Still, I keep asking myself why something that feels so effortless can also feel so improper? I am feeling so overwhelmed, so scared, so angry and so lost. I have the answer to my question, yet I am still not sure how to make the answer my reality of everyday life or if I should follow it. It's one thing to know and another to believe it. Since I have not been able to avoid the answer anymore, I am going to have to figure out how, on top of everything, I will learn a new way of handling fear.

I have been so scared to follow my instinct and act on something I have had within me my whole life but has been buried underneath the rules of society, along with being terrified of what I feel is going to bring. It is a moment at the crossroad. I am sitting on the couch. It is another beautiful dark night. This time no flashing car lights are passing by. We live in a quiet little neighborhood next to a farm, so the night is very quiet. I am seeing myself standing in front of two paths, feeling scared and full of doubt. The first path is the way of life as I have known till now. Numbing fear and running away from hard situations producing pain, anger, and frustration as a result. I know it is no longer going to work for me. I could keep going this way with people's sympathy, approval, and understanding, but that is not how I want this journey to go, except it is the known for me. In a weird way, it feels safe, like that is what I am supposed to do or am expected to do. Then there is the second path. In one way, it feels light and beautiful, in addition to feeling so right, natural, and effortless. On the other hand, it is a scary, doubtful, unknown space. So what now? Which one is the right path? It feels like the biggest gamble of my life. The pressure that my baby's life is depending on it isn't helping. I am looking in the direction of the first path. I can see my life flashing in front of me (past, present, future), along with the anxiety getting stronger and fear changing into anger. I want to scream, who in their right mind can make a decision like this! No parent should ever be in a situation like this. The fear level is getting so high that I can feel it in my body. Even though I am sitting on the couch, I feel like I am falling down to my knees. My heartbeat is slowing down. My stomach feels like vomiting. And my brain at this point is starting to shut down because the stress level is so high it can't handle it. I feel myself leaving my body, at the same time feeling guilty, that this is not how a good, strong mother handles the situation. Then comes the moment of surrender in response to survival. A few minutes later, I am able to get myself together enough to explore the second path. I am looking in the direction of that path but can't see anything. It is like a blank canvas. There is no past, future, or fear. I am sitting in stillness for a while trying to understand the meaning of it, analyzing it so I can have a logical explanation for people and me, why I am about to chose this path. Except I can't explain it. Besides the familiar feeling of warmth and knowing what to do, it isn't logical. I feel like it's the right path, yet still doubt myself because of the fear of the unknown.

I stay sitting for little while longer to at least try to name the feeling. A few moments later, I recognize it. It is love. That is also why there hasn't been any fear on that path, because *we can't love and fear at the same time.* After that, I am able to let go of the doubt whether I am making the right decision. *This journey isn't about making fear go away, trying to control cancer, or the outcome of this journey. It is about discovering the power in a loving response to present challenges.*

As with anything new, there have been visits from resistance and fear to test if I practice what I believe. The visits have also come by to strengthen the feeling of love and belief in myself. Every time a lesson has come, it has been overwhelming and exhausting, but big.

Like this one. I am going through the bargaining stage of grief. I have been feeling like I am working so hard to follow my instincts, grow, and do the right thing. Yet lately, I feel like the fight is getting harder and harder. I am exhausted from constantly trying to do better, be better, and thinking if I do all this and chose love, Matthew won't die. As I am driving to a Tai Chi class to learn more meditation techniques to help me be more at peace and in a loving state of mind, all I can think of is how exhausted I feel. I am thinking about all these new ways of living I have been learning and practicing and feel good about that, yet on the other hand, I am questioning if it is good enough. If I do all these things that I feel I am supposed to, is it really going to save Matthew's life? If all these new ways of living keep coming at the speed they have been, am I going to be able to handle it? Am I cracking under pressure? (Which I feel like I am.) Is it supposed to be like this? Am I supposed to feel like this? I don't have answers to any of these questions. All I know is, I wish that for just a little while, maybe a day, I can go back to the old ways of not knowing, feeling, or fighting.

All of a sudden, the lightbulb goes on! I am not tired of learning and feeling; I am tired of fighting and negotiating for Matthew's life. Fighting doesn't feel right, and it isn't. *Fighting is a negative energy and dressed up fear. Fear wants to fight the illness, but in reality, what we fight is what we strengthen.* That's why it feels so exhausting and wrong. I have to let go and surrender the outcome of the future. I guess deep down, I have been bargaining with God that if I do all this, he will keep my baby here.

In Reike (an energy healing) class, the teacher said an interesting thing. "Not always do people get to heal. If they are meant to transition, they will." It was a very hard truth for me to hear (and scary of course), but an essential one for this lesson of fear. It really opened my eyes and helped me surrender. After all, I know by now I can't control cancer or life; I just didn't understand it this deeply.

Every stage of grief has brought me more eye-opening discoveries and ways fear shows up in life that I haven't even recognized before. So I am asking myself the hard question: Am I doing all this to bargain for Matthew's life, or am I doing it to learn to follow the path to love? I know the true answer is hoping that if I do all the right things, Matt will live. I am so exhausted because no matter how good or positive the action has been, deep down, there has been the energy of fight. The minute I surrendered the outcome of cancer (the fight) and focused on the presence of love, I could feel the energy filling up my body. By surrendering, I have switched my thoughts from what I don't want to happen (Matthew to die) to what I want to happen (live in peace, love, and joy). *Whatever we fight or don't want to happen, we automatically strengthen and get.* The fear of outcome has been one part of fear and cancer journey. It hasn't been an easy one to figure out.

What has been even harder for me is finding the answer and dealing with the fear of how daily treatments or procedures are going to affect the quality of Matt's life. This is my depression stage of grief. Mostly because I have always known that this moment, each split second of our life influences our future destiny. What I don't really know is, how do I guide Matthew or teach him about everything he is about to undergo without creating unnecessary fear or giving him too much information? He is only three and a half years old. His world is only supposed to be filled with love, joy, laughter and of course dirt, toys, and playing. The first question I am asking myself is, are we going to be able to do any of these things?

The answer comes to me through silence and listening. We can't play with dirt (doctor's orders), but by watching Matt, I have been able to see we can still laugh, play, and enjoy life the best we can at that given moment.

What about the treatments and procedures? How are they going to affect him in the long run? Just getting through them to survive is not an option for me. No matter how scared I get at times, *cancer is not about surviving, it is about living.* At least for me. *It is about taking every given moment and making the most of it.* At the beginning, each moment was giving to us because of yucky medicine and painful procedures. That is just what we have had to do. So now I have to figure out how to turn something scary, painful, and negative into a good, positive-invigorating move.

For the medicine side, I have explained it in a simple way, how it works and why we have to take it. I have had a help of a French animated movie that went inside the body and showed children how their body works. Luckily, they made one episode specifically about leukemia. It showed how it all starts (beginning symptoms) and how the "bad guys" (Matt calls them that, it's really the white blood cells) are acting inside the body, making it sick. Then it showed the medicine coming into the body, washing out the "bad guys" and the body (in this case a girl) getting healthy and strong. It was so simple, yet so effective. It provided not only understanding for Matt but also peace of mind.

For side effects? I haven't discussed side effects of the medicines, nor have I asked the doctors about them. Matt doesn't know thing like side effects exists. I haven't been sure how his body is going to react to each medicine, so why worry about something that might never happen when there is plenty to worry about now. I am only asking about what I need to look out for to keep him safe. That provides some sense of security and control for me. *We might not be able to choose what or how the medicine works in each body, but we can decide not to put preconceived notions to our child's subconscious given rise to reaction of our child's body to someone else's experience.*

The procedures are a lot harder. I think it is because he can see all these machines that he doesn't understand how they work or what they are going to do to his body as well as looking at all these doctors and nurses filling the room to perform the procedure. Think how overwhelming it must be for a little child. "Do they wonder how many people does it take to give me medicine and get me on my way? What kind of medicine is it? It's not like I have a big body." It is overwhelming for me as a parent to be surrounded by machines and medical staff trying to figure out how to best help my baby and save his life. Where do you even begin to find a solution to this situation? The best way to begin is with me as a parent. I have to figure out what works and what doesn't for us. I know for me understanding how things work puts me at ease. Will that work for Matt? Thankfully, it is working for him too. Each time we talk about what each machine or instrument does, how it helps to get the job done and how it helps his body. When it comes to medical staff, we do the same. We place each doctor or nurse to their particular job (blood draw, anesthesia, procedure, assistance). It really helps eliminate the fear of what they're going to do to his body and how much it is going to hurt.

With each treatment or procedure, we've been getting better and better. We are learning to understand the surroundings, and I have been assuring Matthew I am here if he needs me. I know he will be scared each time, so will I, but the best thing I can do is to assure him I am here and what he is feeling is normal.

Today we have experienced a big shift and change that has had a profound effect on the way we go through procedures and how they will affect the future. Going through another spinal tap, I am realizing for myself that when I am scared about my baby's life or the procedure he is about to undergo, I just need somebody to listen. And I know he needs the same. *We don't need someone else to make things better (they can't) or come up with solutions (that's the doctor's job); just to listen to us, validate that what we are feeling matters or is real—that we are not wrong or weak for feeling that way and that they don't love us any less because of it.*

Love is in listening. Fear is in talking.

From now on, that is exactly what I am going to do for me and for Matt. I am not sure if it is the right thing to do since that is not how I have been raised. We did not talk about feelings growing up. However, since what I know doesn't fully work, I am going to follow my instinct and start teaching myself and my kids about feelings.

We are learning to talk about fear, when and how it comes, how it feels, as well as what to do with it. Most importantly, I am assuring myself and the kids that it is OK to feel scared and I love them and myself no matter what or how we feel. *It is important to include ourself in everything we teach our children; therefore, we can't teach what we don't experience and believe ourselves.*

That has been the biggest life changer. The fear might not go away; it's not supposed to. Our bodies are made to feel that way in scary situations like procedures, but it makes us feel more at ease. *By being heard and validated, it provides a safe, compassionate place for us where we feel loved, eliminating fear and anxiety.*

With each challenge figured out comes another one to be cracked. Listening helps us with our bodies' automatic reaction to fearful situations. Now I am working on how not to put my fears on the kids, especially on Matthew. He has so much to deal with since he is the one to go through everything. How do I recognize my fears from his? Do I even recognize all my fears? I am feeling the guidance point me to absolute silence, meditation. *It is only in absolute silence we can recognize our fears. We need to practice courage to listen in order to know where our fears are coming from.* As doubtful and scared as I am feeling right now about listening, I feel even more afraid of what might happen if I don't. My decision about waking up early in the morning again to meditate and read is becoming easier and easier. I can feel the fear guiding me to love. *All we have to do is feel the intensity of the fear to recognize which path is guiding us to love and which one is driven by ego.* Day after day I am spending as much time in silence as I can, even if it is one minute at a time. Slowly I am starting to recognize, by listening, which fears are mine and how I can separate my fears from his. I can empathize with his fears and guide him through his while staying compassionate with myself about mine. Understanding all this is also helping me find acceptance.

Even though I have known better, sometimes I have still been so afraid to silence myself to hear the answer, because I am not sure if I can handle the truth. At times I have been feeling so afraid of the truth I figured if I talk about something else, I can avoid the inevitable. Whether the talk has been out loud or inside my head, it doesn't matter; any distraction would do. Same as any other lesson. This one keeps coming back in different situations to affirm only one thing: that not only have I been able to handle the truth, *the reality is always better than the assumption created through fear.*

The end of treatment is here. I have been ready for everything, I thought. I have known about the fear of life without medicine and grieving, and I am feeling confident I can avoid all that through knowing and mastering the influences, especially the present moment. For the most part, I am. Until about now when Matthew's face is starting to get covered with rash. I can feel I am about to really affirm the lesson about talking (fear) versus silence (love). All of a sudden, all these feelings are running through my body. Not to mention I have lost a friend to cancer three days after Matthew's last chemo. At this point, my body feels like a dumping ground for any possible feeling. A storm is whirling inside my body. I can feel emotions running, crashing, and exploding in every single cell. I am crying, laughing, and experiencing sadness, happiness, pain, pleasure, confusion, clarity, along with feeling completely hopeless all at the same time.

I am going through the grieving stage over the end of the treatment, which at this point I can do in a matter of hours, as well as grieving the loss of my friend, so when this unexpected condition starts to present itself, I am starting to crack under the pressure of it all.

Am I ready to figure out what is causing the rash? Absolutely not. So I am starting to talk out loud and inside my head about every possibility, like cat, food, fall allergies, sweating, bed bugs etc., numbing the fear of my assumptions that this is how cancer is showing us it's back. I can't talk anymore. Time to face the truth. My instinct is guiding me to silence once again, helping me find my answer through listening

I know it is Matthew's body cleansing him from the chemo, yet the little doubt keeps creeping in. He is asking about his rash as well, expressing his unease. Even though I feel mostly confident about why the rash is here, I ask him if it would make him feel better to call the doctor. He says yes. Calling the doctor makes us feel much better even though they couldn't guarantee 100 percent over the phone that it is what that is. They did mention that a lot of kids break out after stopping the medicine. For me, it is a confirmation that it's not about eliminating fear out of our life. *It is about creating a moment of stillness to find the answers through the silence of our heart and not through the loudness of our words while compassionately honoring ourselves and our children's feelings.*

Consequently, I am recognizing that it is only when I conquer and become conscious of my fears I can be a better parent for my children and guide them through any life experiences (even heartbreaking ones) with love. That will guarantee not only a successful future but an authentic destiny, along with connection between me and my children. Like Gerald Jampolsky said,

We cannot love when we fear.
—G. Jampolsky

Understanding all the ways fear shows up in our life, as well as our decisions, gives us the necessary courage to love our children without the condition or control of what the situation is or what the future outcome is going to bring. That is the utmost breakthrough for me that I will forever be very grateful for.

SUMMARY

- You cannot love when you feel fear.
- Believe you are good enough.
- Focus on what you want, not on what you don't want.
- Remember, fear wants to fight the illness, but whatever you fight or don't want, you strengthen.
- Recognize all the ways fear shows up in your life.
- Have the courage to say the facts about the illness (age appropriate) without putting your feeling of fear behind it. Let your child decide if it is scary for him/her.
- Validate your feelings of fear and your child/children's through listening, and know it's OK to be scared.
- Talk about scary procedures and treatments.
- Don't blame yourself or feel like you have to make things better. Assure your child that whatever he/she feels is appropriate as well as important, along with telling them your love is unconditional, and do the same for yourself.
- Find answers through the silence of your heart, not through the loudness of your words.

Expectation

What if I would exclude judgments and opinions of others?

The pressure is on!

That is all I can feel driving to the emergency room. I don't know what we are going to find out or what awaits ahead of us which is terrifying, but all I can feel is the importance of the first impression. I have been in hospitals, understood how they work and why, as well as what to expect when you walk in the door. Stuff like how the emergency room looks, that doctors and nurses work there, how the visit is going to go, but Matthew and Jojo have never been to the hospital. For them it is going to be a new experience. *Kids have no facts, no information, or prospect of what is going to go on once you walk through the door of the hospital. First impression sets the tone for the whole journey.* They are so innocent. Their life is just beginning, and until this moment, it has been filled with happy memories.

The Dora exploring trip is giving me an idea. What if I can make every experience in the hospital into a fun exploration? Yes, it does sound wrong, but sometimes I am not able to handle the scary reality of things. This sounds like something I can handle. Plus kids have the gift to make anything magical. They can make even the most unexpected thing into an unforgettable experience. So I am going to listen. *We need to listen to our inner child, hush the experienced grown-up, and go with the children's vision of how the world should be. It will always bring the results we want.* Hospitals should be happy places where we go to feel better.

As we are getting closer to the hospital, the kids start to ask questions about what we are going to do, how the hospital is going to look, whether we have to stay there for long, etc. I am keeping my answers as simple as I can. Since they know how a doctor's office looks, I am using it as a starting point. Describing that the hospital will have more doctors and nurses, will be bigger, and have beds satisfies their curiosity for the moment.

Right before pulling in, we see Daddy. He is driving in front of us. Great, let me use him as a distraction. He is meeting us by the ER entrance. It is giving me a moment to gather myself without the kids noticing, because they are so excited to see Daddy's car. This is what I am talking about when I say they can make every moment magical. They are happy, laughing and screaming, "Daddy's car. Daddy, Daddy, Daddy over here! We are right behind you!" (Not that he can hear us, but they believe he can.) They are so beautifully in the moment, enjoying every second they get. Experiencing their presence is giving me even more courage to follow my plan of making everything a fun exploration. *Finding courage to follow our instinct and set our own expectations, by watching our children be present and enjoy each moment they get not thinking about the future, will inspire us to do the same!*

Right after we walk into the emergency room, we get called in. It is in that moment I know things aren't looking too good. After all, the wait is usually at least a couple of hours. We go through the basics—blood pressure, weight, etc.—and after we are done, they are taking us to our room. Let our exploring begin. I am pointing out the fact Matthew is visiting in style, having his own room, TV, bed, and nice doctors and nurses to chat with. On the inside, I am terrified and want to run and scream.

Things are moving along. Matt gets his blood drawn (when the magical bee takes a little bit of his special blood) and heading for an x-ray. Riding on the bed to get there is the coolest thing ever, and I am making sure it is even cooler than that, trying to keep the focus on the ride, not on what is coming. His face is lit up with excitement and joy. After all, it's not every day you get to ride in the bed.

We are here, at the castle (x-ray room). It is time to leave the riding bed to sit in the king's throne (x-ray chair) so we can take special pictures of the insides of your body pumpkin, I say. I am assuring him, along with the people who work there, that it won't hurt, that it is just the coolest thing ever, and if he wants, we can see the pictures later. That spikes his curiosity. After all, for him, it is something outside of this world; it's not every day you get to see inside of yourself. I can see on his face how he is trying to solve the mystery of something like this even being possible. It is reassuring me I am on the right track. *Focusing on creating the experience being unique brings love and compassion into being, allowing the seeds to grow in our thoughts, anticipating positive expectations and outcomes.*

After the x-ray, we are ready to return to the ER, where we are going to wait for a couple of hours to get the results. Longest couple of hours of my life. I am using the bathroom for much needed breakdowns and keep asking if they are able to tell us anything. Finally, they say, "You are getting admitted overnight, and Matthew is going to get a transfusion."

As soon as I can somewhat process the news, with a helpful bathroom break, I am able to get excited about riding the bed again. This time Jojo (sister) is able to experience the coolness of riding in the bed as well. They are both sitting on the bed enjoying a ride, only this time there is a little bit of doubt about the future. What is going to happen when we get to the room? I can see it in their eyes, and I can feel it in myself. Quickly, what can I say to bring us all to the present moment? Questions always work "Hey, guys, how cool is this? Have you ever thought there is a riding bed and you would ever ride one?" Like magic, they start to answer and get in the present moment, realizing what an awesome experience this is. Jojo is saying how cool it will be to tell her classmates.

We are in our new room and settling in to receive the miraculous new blood with the aim of feeling better. The hotel room (hospital room) is spectacular. We are embracing the wonderful accommodations: couch, TV, bed all in one room, plus eating in bed—don't get that at home. Even though we are all scared in some way, we try to focus on the positive side of things. Not only that, at this point, I know it's not going to be a quick fix, so feeling comfortable and safe in the hospital setting as much as we can is a must for me. After we are done settling in and Jojo feels safe about where Matthew and I are going to spend the night, they are ready to go home and get some rest. My friend left shortly after, and it is just me and Matt.

We lie in bed holding tight to each other without words. He is so exhausted, and I am afraid to say anything to try to make things better because I know I would be making promises I might not be able to keep. At the same time, I am taking in how close, safe, and loving we feel. It has a powerful message, and I can feel it is a good aspect for our future. One of my biggest fears is for Matt or Jojo to feel alone or not loved. Until this point in my life, I thought I had to be a know-and-do-it all in order for my kids to feel loved. This experience is showing me that all I have to do is show up the way I am (not trying to be stronger, better, smarter) and we will figure out the rest together. *Number one and the most important expectation to have, is to show up for right now, no matter how imperfect we feel, and do our best at any given moment without feeling guilty we should be, do, or know more!*

Matthew is sleeping. I am sitting on the couch by the window looking out, trying to process all the information we have been given. My conclusion is the realization that this is going to be a ride of a lifetime and the best thing I can do is to be, surrender the future, and pay attention to the signs along the way.

It is morning, the sun is shinning through the window. In a strange way I feel it represents the bright new beginning. Because I believe behind every cloud is a sunshine. Today we are doing the bone-marrow test, and we will confirm the diagnosis (our cloud).

It is leukemia. Everything is happening so fast. Surgery to implant the medi port, paperwork to sign all permissions for treatment, clinical-trial questions, and our first round of chemo. We need to stay in the hospital for a week, they say. Every night I am finding myself sitting on the couch trying to understand the meanings of whatever has happened that day. With each day, it is getting harder to stay in our fairyland since every hour is filled with more and more pain and not so much feeling better. We are doing our best to focus on the good in things and make the most of the minutes that are pain free.

A few days went by, and I desperately want to figure out, how I am going to do this. I am physically and mentally exhausted after a couple of days. And the treatment is going to be three years and four months long. Even though we have had a good attitude, along with a couple of breathtaking moments by this time, my thoughts are going back to the known picture of how cancer should look like. Going through nursing school, I have seen children's oncology units. It was a place filled with fear and sadness. All my other memories associated with cancer are filled with fear, sadness, and death too. One of the girls in our class died of ovarian cancer at the age of sixteen. My grandfather died of cancer right after I came to the United States. Allynn's father (the kid's grandfather) died of cancer. A couple of my parents' friends died of cancer. So every time I hear the word *cancer* all I can see is fear, sadness, exhaustion, death, and defeat. I think that's why part of me wants to know how it's going to end. All I can see at this point is my baby dying. The other side of me is saying, what kind of mother thinks like that?

Thankfully, in my nights of silence, I can see and feel that whatever my memories have been so far is not going to be my experience with cancer this time. I have to change how I think and act, but since the known to me is too much to handle, change feels like a better option anyway. As easy as it is, in my thoughts, I know taking actions with following through is going to be *the work* of my lifetime. It's going to take everything I got and then some to grow, change, and break the pattern.

The first step is to make a choice and visualize how I want the next few years to look. *To create our vision of how our new life should be and setting our own expectations takes more courage than living up to the vision of others about how we should live our life. It will empower us and our child!* How do I even begin to visualize greatness in the dark, the hardest time of my life? How do I make a choice like that? How do I go from the known to the unknown? Where is the courage to do all this going to come from?

Well, for starters, the fact that I can't handle things as I know them helps. I am accepting that our life is the way it is and the fact that cancer is here whether we want it or not. *In order for things to change, our intentions have to come from a place of acceptance. The minute we accept life as it is change will effortlessly enter and, based on our intentions, will smoothly guide us toward our goal.* Also, I have been incredibly blessed with being able to see the good side of things, no matter how unfortunate life gets. That, along with high hopes and guidance from instinct of how to go about my life differently, has been my driving force to a better life. It has been my support behind every courageous act toward the unexplainable unknown. *Know we have the ability to see the good in the bad if we chose to and we can change our life by following our instinct!*

A few weeks went by, and I am experiencing an *Aha* moment. Like probably every parent out there, I have been expecting Matthew to be sad and tired, not feeling good or in a lot of pain. I have been expecting my old remembrance to show up in Matthew's journey. To my surprise, I am disappointed, in a very good way. Matthew is Matthew. He has been happy, running, laughing, and wanting to do everything that he was used to doing. I am very confused and don't know what to make of it, and it is somewhat scary. I have been visualizing and hoping for outcomes like this, so why does it feel scary? Why, when I get what I want, am I not able to fully enjoy it? Is it supposed to be like this? I am really not sure yet, given I am fairly new to stepping into the unknown, but I am very determined to get the result I want—Matthew surviving cancer and living life to the fullest each second, not giving into fear by postponing life for a later more convenient time.

My thoughts and feelings are going back and forth, saying follow the new way one second, fall into the known the next. On top of the grieving process, it feels like a storm and tornado inside my body. This particular doctor's visit, I am asking the nurse if this response is normal. "Do you have kids that act like this? Is this a good thing or bad thing that he has so much energy?" (Matthew is not in the room) As I am asking, I am feeling so scared of what the answer will be, yet I am looking for the reassurance that it is normal and that it's not that "quiet before the storm." There is a silent moment after I ask the question that lasts about a second or two, but it is one of the scariest. What if they say it is not normal? What if they confirm that he is dying (my biggest fear), that he only has a couple of days? They can't take my baby. That is *my* baby. My kids are the reason I was born. I am standing on the outside, but inside I feel myself falling down to my knees, curling up into a ball, throwing up, and screaming for help. At the same moment I realize that it is the fear of the new, unknown life. I have been so used to the opposite reactions to cancer (sadness, no energy) that this doesn't feel natural. Not at first anyway. Even though it is what I want and wish for, resistance is challenging me to see if I will be courageous enough to stick with the plan. *Resistance will always show up when we're following our dream and embracing change. The bigger the dream, the stronger the resistance. But at the end, the reward is priceless and worth it!* This is my opportunity to follow my dream. I have to surrender trying to control life or the end result. Only by doing that will I be able step closer to living my new life. It's moments like this I am most grateful for, because even though the fear will always sneak up on me (and it's ugly for a little while), I can always see the answer coming from love as well as find the courage to follow through. The pressure of my baby's life depending on my every action forces me to face previously impossible fears and have the courage to create a new destiny. Of course the nurse cannot tell me anything or confirm anything, so at the same time, as she's answering, I am giving up that need to know what is going to be. We always need a couple of confirmations as human beings about one subject, and I am getting mine about trying to control anything.

So from this moment on, I am making the decision that I will listen to my baby boy, and since I have no idea how to go through his journey, the best thing for everybody is for me to see how he chooses to go through it. I have learned to trust my new way of life and get comfortable with enjoying all the good life has to offer, along with the bad. Matthew keeps amazing me with his great attitude and zest for life, and for the first time ever, I have been able to enjoy being without the fear of something bad coming. You know when people say, "Oh, things are going well for you? Be on lookout. Something bad is going to happen."

Matthew's expectations haven't changed much since we first found out he has cancer. He has been happy, energetic, and active through the treatment. I have been able to find guts to follow him and make laughter with joy part of our every day. After all, he is the one feeling everything.

No longer do I care to live up to what I know (that is too scary) or the expectations of how we should do things and how we should live our life with cancer. The only person who gets to decide which way we go on this journey is going to be Matthew, nobody else. As hard as it is at time to live in the unknown, I know it would have been harder to live with what I knew from old experiences or expectations of others. *Running from pain only strengthens it, which is a lot harder than to walk through the pain. By setting our own expectations, we eliminate going through other people's experiences and pain.* Despite dirty looks, scornful judgments, misunderstanding, as well as the lack of ability to see our point of view, we are persistently holding in our arms the greater purpose for everything that is being sent our way. It is giving us the freedom to decide what the right decision for our family is. With that, we keep cycling through hospital hallways, having fun playing on the rooftop, dancing, running, swimming, laughing, and playing hard while being grateful for every given moment. It doesn't matter whether the occasion is big (Disney) or small (ordinary day), sad (chemo, spinal) or happy (turning the TV to 100 percent volume like it's the coolest thing ever). We live through it all fully honoring each encounter, knowing it is for our greater good to help us find life's purpose and spread love to make the world a better place.

I am becoming aware of and am able to learn back from my babies what I once knew myself, which is, *by believing we have what we need within, we all have the power of a beautiful choice to do something different, something outside of a box.*

My kids have been such powerful teachers to me and they are only four and seven years old. Matthew's zest for life and his courage to be who he wants to be and to do what he wants to do with his life despite other people's expectations of him is reinforcing my courage. Jojo's unconditional love, compassion, and ability to forgive, along with her courage to listen and patiently wait for her turn while giving up what she needs for her brother, is making me a better, more compassionate parent and human. My babies are the reason that today we have the life we have. They have taught me how to get to know who they are instead of telling them who they should be based on my fears and imperfections. How to set expectations instead of limitations. How to parent out of love instead of fear. The only thing I have to do in order to be a good parent is to encourage them to use the abilities they already have within so they can initiate their destiny and do the same for myself. *Learn to set expectations instead of limitations!*

What started as my weakness (not being able to handle hard times) is being the greatest gift. So many times people tell me how strong I am (seeing me happy), but it is the other way around. For me personally, it takes a lot more strength to be sad, unhappy, and scared than it ever takes to enjoy life. Us enjoying life gives Matthew the strength to go through what he has to go through, feeling loved and safe. The greatest gift I am giving to my children is showing up as I am, with all my imperfections, insecurities, and weaknesses, not trying to be better. It has been tough, especially at the beginning, plus I don't always get it right, but I can recognize my mistakes and see *a beautiful choice* how to fix it. *Recognize that our weaknesses are actually our strengths. In that we will always feel the right guidance for our family, in addition to getting the results we want!*

SUMMARY

- Look at things through children's eyes so you can see where they are coming from and how they understand it.
- Try to make new scary experiences into a magical adventure, especially at the beginning.
- Less is more. Don't feel like you have to explain everything, especially if you don't know how. Just being is enough.
- Only make promises you can keep.
- Set up your own expectations based on your family's experiences, not based on what you know from past or preconceived notions of someone else.
- Watch and listen to your children to figure out their expectations.

- Support your children's expectations even if you don't agree or it doesn't make sense. It honors who they are and empowers them.
- Practice courage to get out of your comfort zone to create a new vision for your life.
- Forgive yourself for not doing it right, even if you knew better, and keep trying. Kids always appreciate our effort.
- Take time to break down. It takes a strong parent to be vulnerable.
- Feeling of joy, happiness, love, and excitement is the best medicine and the only thing kids want from you.
- Make sure your eyes light up around your children.
- Embrace having the time of your life, leaving guilt or thinking you should be sad, unhappy, or overwhelmed behind.
- Use the journey through cancer to stop worrying about other people's judgments and opinions. It's only their insecurity, as well as lack of courage to be or do what they would like.
- Most of all, live fully through each moment you are given.

Ego

What if cancer would give me the gift to live my life like I have always wanted, without limitations?

I am trembling, vomiting, falling down to my knees, curled up on the floor, screaming for someone to save me on the inside while at the same time paying attention to the road on the outside, as we are driving to the hospital because of another nosebleed. I am trying to smile as much as I can and keep the conversation going so the kids won't feel so much pain and fear, but they are. It is yet another very stressful morning for all of us. Let me go back and start from the beginning.

We are waking up. Every morning I remember to say quickly what I am grateful for before I open my eyes, thank you for the gift of another day. I turn around, open my eyes, to see Matthew and feel even more grateful for him being alive, next to me, and ready to embrace anything this day has to offer. Only what I see is Matthew's fearful face looking at the bed that is covered with his blood. He is scared of what is going on. Why is his nose bleeding so much? At the same time, he is afraid I will get mad at him for getting it all over the bed. I am feeling the fear right now. My fear wants to attack and say, why didn't you wake me up when you knew your nose was bleeding? At this point, I know to let the feeling pass, it's the fear talking, and not react to it. However, I do need a few seconds to gather myself.

"Are you OK, baby?" I ask him. He replies by saying yes and sorry about the bed at the same time. "Don't worry about the bed," I say. "Can you go to the bathroom, please? Mommy will be right there." I am giving myself a minute to let the feeling of agonizing fear pass. As I look at the pillows covered with Matthew's blood, I am working on staying in the present moment while the memories of the last nosebleed, where we almost lost Matthew, are creeping into my thoughts. I feel collected enough to face what awaits me in the bathroom. Matthew is standing over the toilet, and when he sees me, he looks up and steps aside. I am left with the vision of what looks like a murder scene.

There is so much blood in the toilet and on Matthew's face, body, and pajamas as well as every spot around him. His face is filled with fear and an enormous amount of panic. My body is flooding with fear once again. He is looking at me, and I feel his plea for help and understanding. I am feeling hopeless without any ideas why this is happening or how to stop it. At the same time (due to a lot of moments like this), my body is having a three-way conversation even as I am trying to stop the bleeding and talk to Matthew so he doesn't feel alone. I don't multitask, but moments like this make me wonder if I should. No, it never works.

Even in stressful moments, it can only be one thought, one action, one act of love at a time in order for us to be helpful. It might seem like it is all happening at once, but in reality, it is just happening really fast. In split seconds, my thoughts and feelings are changing from one to another. When I am finally able to observe the slow motion of everything, I can see it. It looks like it is all going on at once because our body's action is slow to scary situations while our thoughts and feelings travel at the speed of light.

I am holding a sheet of toilet paper up to Matthew's nose, trying to stop the bleeding and stay calm doing it when all of a sudden, he starts to push my hand away because he doesn't like the bloody part of the tissue touching back on his nose. I am losing it. I am yelling at him to let me put the toilet paper back by his nose. Even as the words of fear are coming out, I feel so bad because I know he is really scared too and this doesn't make it any easier. The difference today is, I can explain to him why Mommy is yelling, that it isn't anything he is doing, that Mommy is just scared. By explaining and apologizing to him, I am showing him that *we might not always get things right and that is OK because we are imperfect human beings. By saying sorry, to*

ourselves first, we treat ourselves and others with kindness, consideration,
and benevolence, which are true acts of love.

Looking at him, I see his face has an expression of gratefulness. Not as much about the apology as about the fact that I am scared as he is and I am not sure about what is going to happen. It is validating everything he is feeling, and even though at this time we are not successful at stopping the bleeding, our success is in connecting with each other and being compassionate despite our fears. I ask him to hold the tissue while I go to page the doctor, and as soon as I finish the phone call, I come back to sit with him in the bathroom.

I am back. For a few seconds, the bathroom is filled with silence as we are holding on to each other. When I am able gather enough courage, I am asking Matthew if he is scared. I know and feel he has been, but hearing it out loud is a whole different experience. It makes it real. It is a point when I can no longer pretend he is resilient while convincing myself he is fine and this experience is not really affecting him. He is saying he has been really scared, yet when I ask him if he remembers the last time his nose was bleeding, he says no. I think his body might, and that is why he has been super scared. We stay sitting quietly for another couple of minutes, still waiting for the nosebleed to stop. In the silence of the moment my memory is going through the flashbacks of our last experience.

It happened a few months into treatment. The bleeding started slowly in the evening and stopped a few minutes later. I was alarmed, called the doctor, and confirmed I needed to watch Matthew overnight. Given I haven't had any previous experience with nosebleeds, I was able to get through the first twelve hours somewhat calm. I stayed up most of the night watching my baby sleep, making sure his nose didn't start bleeding again, and it didn't. Not until the morning when he had another little bleed. We got dressed and headed to the hospital for a blood check. At that time, his chemo was so intense that there was no guarantee of what was going on inside his body, so we needed to make sure he had enough platelets to stop any potential bleeding. His platelets level was very low. Consequently, we got admitted to the hospital and scheduled for a platelets transfusion. As we were settling in our lovely hotel room (hospital room), his nose started to bleed again. Only this time it was gushing out of him like crazy. It was like someone turned on a faucet in his head. I was so grateful it wasn't like this at home. I don't think I would be able to handle that or know what to do. I thanked God for letting it happen the way it did, with us surrounded by people that knew how to help my baby.

Even though I was grateful for being in the hospital, I was freaking out and terrified on the inside. *Why is this happening? Is it ever going to stop? Is this it? Is God going to take my baby away? Are these the last moments we're ever going to spend together? Is this the last time I get to hold my baby?* All these questions were running through my head while I was trying to get a hold of myself so I could be there for Matthew. If these were the last moments we were spending together I wanted to remember them. I wanted Matthew to feel *so* loved, and I knew if I feared the future outcome or try to fight whatever was coming at us, I wouldn't be able to love him in the present moment. Fear, pain, and fight had to go away immediately. I was guided to Eckhart Tolle's words:

> **If you lose yourself in every thought and every emotion, you are totally identified with form and therefore in the grip of EGO.**
>
> **—Eckhart Tolle**

Understanding what that meant, plus the insurmountable pain with fear, helped me let go, surrender every thought and every emotion, making room for love. I was able to let my negative thoughts pass without resisting them or feeling guilty I was thinking them. *In bloodcurdling situations, when our child is in a life-threatening situation, ego makes decisions based on comparison (how good we fight for our kids) and what we don't want the outcome to be, eliminating any present moment, therefore love! Fight makes our child feel alone and unloved!* Our fears are based on previous painful experiences that might not necessarily have anything to do with present situation as well as collected knowledge of someone else's experiences, therefore producing the result we don't want or are the most afraid of (universe doesn't recognize *don't*). *Fight removes any possibility for compassion or connection!* When we fight, it's based on fearful emotion. We defend unfair circumstances, lack of _____, and our right to feel the way we feel. *Fight is negative energy, a form of resistance, and for that reason, it brings into being negative, unwanted consequences!*

Did I want to scream at everybody to do something more? To move faster, to only pay attention to my baby and accuse them of not being able to do their job better because they still hadn't been able to stop Matthew's nose from bleeding? Of course, my ego is as good as the next person. Being able to distinguish the outcome helped me bring the ego response to a halt. It was always in the back of my head. Only I acknowledge its presence without attaching myself to any thought, emotion, or form (my children, especially Matthew), resulting in the ego dropping itself away due to me no longer seeking to find myself through it. *Not reacting to egotistical thoughts or resisting them, they go away on their own, unlocks room for love!* I was able to fill my heart with love and just be fully present with Matthew. I focused on what was being done to help Matthew as well as how I wanted to go through this experience. I wanted to enjoy any given moment I had with him without conditioning how should that moment look. I felt peace and connection. We played memory games, watched TV, and muddled (stands for "cuddling with Mommy") when we could. I wasn't modest on the amount of kisses I gave him or expressions of how much I loved him. Yes, the ego was always at the back of my head telling me how I was wrong, how I should feel scared and sad, how I shouldn't kiss him or tell him how much I loved him because that was going to bring bad ending to the situation, but I just watched the thoughts pass by without reacting to them since I knew that reacting to ego is a no-win situation. Me expressing my love for Matthew was only going to be a good thing. No matter what the end result was going to be, I knew him feeling loved was the only thing that mattered.

It took over four hours and a couple of transfusions to stop the nosebleed. We finished up by vomiting buckets of blood in view of the fact that whatever blood couldn't leak out the nose got swallowed to the stomach. We were both so relieved it was over and just kept holding on to each other, lying in a hospital bed for a while.

Now here I am, sitting on the bathroom floor years later, watching the blood gushing out his nose, and trying to stay calm, it is a lot more challenging. I am recognizing that the situation is different; we are done with chemo, and his numbers are good. Still, the ego keeps running doubtful thoughts. What if it isn't different? What if we are not going to be so lucky this time?

Even though it is harder this time around, I am able to just watch the thoughts pass by without reacting to them much, except the one yelling incident. It took about ten minutes for his bleeding to stop but it felt like a lifetime. We are getting dressed so we can head for the hospital.

The car ride is bringing up its own set of scary thoughts and feelings. The feeling of relief has stopped, and my body is getting flooded with every other emotion that has been on hold while under pressure. That is why I feel the trembling, vomiting, falling-down-to-my-knees, screaming-for-help, curling-up-on-the-floor reaction.

What I am trying to say is this: *Separating ourselves from ego helps us detach from our child, and we are able to see things and situations with a more objective point of view (not take it personally), able to compassionately guide our children through their experiences, supporting their point of view (how they want to go through it) and who they are!* Unfortunately, it doesn't mean the ego is forever gone. Our thoughts, feelings, and association with form (cancer) come for daily visits to test our ability to recognize it but not react on it.

I watch my thoughts and practice not reacting to them, sometimes a hundred times a day. I watch my ego try to make my body sick in order to strengthen itself when it can't win any other way, and till I can recognize it is ego, it wins. Whether it is my heart skipping beats, anxiety, depression, or physical exhaustion, at the end of the day, it is just my ego trying to take over me. There are so many ways through which the ego will try to find stronger identity, especially when it comes to parenting children with a life-threatening illness. *It takes a wider open mind to be acquainted with all the possible ways the ego will try to get us and win!* Unfortunately, or thankfully (however you want to look at it), we are presented with plenty of opportunities, given our children are going through life-threatening illness, to practice the separation from our ego. *Overcoming ego is providing us with the gift of a lifetime: experiencing unconditional love! It is only when we are able to go passed the ego and meet our true self are we able to feel true love!* Like I said, ego functions through fear. Fear and love can't coexist. *If we are in any way, even a little bit, doubtful or fearful, love is only experienced through our logic, not through our hearts!*

The ego has been kicking my butt. Whether it has been through side effects like influenza A, pneumonia, or routine procedures like blood work, chemo, and spinal tap, every time I watch my baby go through painful, scary conditions, looking at the tears running down his face, the ego challenges me by filling my brain with upsetting, unwanted thoughts and feelings. It tries to prevent me from compassion and connection with Matthew, following with flooding my body with almost unbearable emotions. The difference is, what used to take me hours, days, and sometimes even weeks only takes me minutes now. The intensity is the same, but the length and power are almost nonexistent.

Understanding ego hasn't been just to help me deal with day-to-day disputes. It is part of it. My main goal for parenting my children through cancer has been to stay being their mommy and make them feel loved. If I haven't recognized the ego and its need to attach itself to thought, I would have never been able to do that. Why? For the reason that ego would always make me feel not enough. I am not enough, I don't know enough, I don't do enough, I am not perfect enough, I am not strong enough, which are all fear-based responses, creating a fighting mode to protect and defend my babies, making them feel all alone and unlovable. *Where there is fear, there is no room for love, and people will always feel less than and not loved!* Giving into ego would make me tell my kids what to do based on my needs instead of guiding them based on theirs. Ego would make me compare myself, along with our situation, to others, hoping to be better or better off, in addition to being right, missing the importance of compassion, which is only possible through love. Ego would make the whole thing about my doing, how strong I am, how much I do for my kids, how much I know, how well I handle things, how much I have to go through (looking for approval and compassion through fear), not leaving any room for being, compassion, and love. Ego would have never allowed me to see that it is my baby going through all the pain, not me. Anything I have been hurting about is created by the ego; it is only in my thoughts.

It is not my body that has been hurting every day. I am not the one needing a break from the painful procedures and yucky medicine. It isn't me who can't get away from scary nightmares due to side effects of the medicine. My life hasn't changed much. I chose to be a parent, and that is what I want to do.

Ego would never allow peace because peace comes from a place of abundance, not scarcity. Ego would never let me see the manifestations of Matthew's pains accumulated through the horrifying sight of procedures, feeling from chemo, scary circumstances, and intimidating machines. The way pain shows up in children, the ego would take the warning sign personally and make it all about me. To better explain, here is one example how pain shows.

Nosebleed has stopped, blood count is good, and we have a chance to talk about the morning, expressing our feelings over our special lunch. After every doctor's visit, we go to our special secret restaurant with an amazing view of the world (tenth floor cafeteria). Jojo is able to tell me how scared she was about Matthew and him dying while he went to the bathroom. Matthew is concerned about dying too, and it really left a mark on him. At this time (after a lot of soul-searching), I am able to talk about my fears in front of the kids, so I am sharing how scared I was too. Talking about it helps, but I know it will take time for all of us to go through the grieving process.

Right now we are trying to let go of what we will need to do and we are trying to just be.

We are leaving the hospital parking lot. I mention we need to stop at our family doctor's office on the way home. It will just be an in and out. When we get there, we have to wait for a couple of minutes for the receptionist to come in order for me to buy what I need. The kids are playing with the toys (very nicely together), just being loud. I am asking them to be a little quieter. A few minutes go by, I am asking them to be quiet again, only they are not even trying. I have a feeling what it is about, so I am surrendering what people might say, get what I need, and we are ready to leave.

In the car I am explaining how their behavior was disrespectful and that being loud in the doctor's office is not an appropriate behavior (which they know). I am trying so hard to hold it together, between my PMS and my pain, not lashing out at my babies because I know their behavior is all about the pain. *Children are just starting to learn about feelings, so they let them out however the feeling needs to come out at that particular time. Pain in children comes out in one of these ways: loudness, teasing, disrespect, and annoying, disruptive, or self-destructive behavior. It is our job to teach them otherwise, but first we have to learn it ourselves!* The ego takes these behaviors personally punishing the child for it. By separating from the ego I am able to teach my kids versus punish them. I am explaining to them how them acting up on their pain (being loud) became disrespectful behavior. Every time we act on our pain we will only cause more pain back at us as well as others. We are going over ways of how to recognize pain and how to deal with our pain in a respectful manner, making it work for us, staying true to ourselves, while staying respectful to others.

Contrary to the pain staying in, quiet and not dealt with, the ego rewards the child's behavior (good girl/boy), which consequently results in unhappiness, anxiety, depression, loneliness, and the feeling of giving up in children.

Recognizing how ego shows up and manipulates every thought, decision, or action is my most practiced influence. Sometimes I get it right, and sometimes I don't, but either way, I win. Being familiar with ego creates an opportunity for better parenting. Even though I get it wrong at times I am able to think about it and explain to the kids why I think or react the way I do. This opens new doors for the kids to recognize how ego plays a role in their life. A lot of people think I have been in denial or am not dealing with the reality of the situation. The fact is, I am too busy and quiet trying to comprehend the guidance and find words to explain it. On the outside, I might look put together, laughing and knowing what I am doing at all times. On the inside, I am going through a storm of a lifetime.

The times I am not with my babies are spent clearing up the storm by understanding and dealing with everything that is going on, in addition to clearing the misunderstanding about the state we parent out of, while trying to see the sunshine behind the cloud. It has been the most fruit-producing experience (getting results I have always wanted). And the most effective crash course in life. I am forever grateful for everything I have learned and for the person I have become. I am now the parent I have forever wanted to be and have the connection with my babies I have always wanted to have. Love fills our every day; no matter what the circumstance is thus, I can't wish for more.

SUMMARY

- Understanding how ego works helps you gain an objective point of view.
- Separating yourselves from ego opens doors for love and compassion, producing the result you want.
- Not reacting to thoughts of ego helps you stay true to yourselves.
- Ego doesn't allow peace, listening, teaching, or feeling of being enough because it functions on scarcity and fear.
- Ego equals fight, lack of __, unfairness, need to be right, therefore producing negative results.
- Recognizing how ego places a role in your relationship with children helps you detach from your child, opening a space to get to know them and see how they are feeling about what is going on, how they deal with what is going on, as well as how they would like their journey to look based on what they need and who they are.
- Separating from ego helps you stay Mommy/Daddy (something all kids need the most) versus fighter, doctor, or robot.
- Separating from ego allows you to just be and enjoy every moment you get with your babies, surrendering control over outcome.
- Being aware of ego guides you to becoming excellent teachers as opposed to dictators.
- Ego always compares itself to others.

- Ego prevents you from seeing how pain manifests itself by taking the behavior personally.
- Ego will never allow connection and love with your babies.
- Ego will, at all times, leave you feeling exhausted, overwhelmed, not enough, alone, lost, confused, guilty, unfulfilled, unhappy, scared, bad, desperate, wrong, etc.

Present Moment

**What if the only thing I have to do today is
the one thing I am doing right now?**

By now few weeks went by. Things are settling to our new normal. I am relieved that, thanks to Matthew, I have the permission to be happy and enjoy life as it is now. We continue to swim, go for our walks, visit parks, and play with friends. We do those activities a little differently, but we are able to do them. Yet something inside me keeps nagging me about living in the present moment (you know that little voice that never leaves you even when nobody is looking or listening). I am thinking I have been doing pretty good, but clearly my little voice doesn't think so. I am thankful for it and learned to listen to it even if it does not make sense at the time. I know I will understand what I need to understand when the time is right. All I need to do now is to go with my instinct without doubting it. *The power of the present moment is in being able to listen to our instinct and follow it by action. As long as we stay in the now, we are able to listen to our instinct through presence of love and not attaching ourselves to outcome!*

Living in the present moment for a little while hasn't been that hard (given the situation), but as the weeks go by, it is getting harder and harder. Life is getting back to normal (new normal), and our everyday routine is back to full speed and then some. All the stay-at-home moms know what I am talking about. From the minute I get up, I don't stop moving, doing anything from preparing five meals a day to doing dishes after those meals, to laundry, cleaning, shopping, playdates, schoolwork, and the list goes on and on. Now we have doctors visits, medicine, and the side effects of it to add into our day without obtaining any extra time. My heart goes out to the working moms. I don't even know how they squeeze a job in all that or how they do it all. So yes, it was easy to be in the present moment the first week because none of those things mattered, but life does go on, and I have to do all these things and not just for a week or two.

So how do I go from the future to now? How do I make the shift when the habit of living in the future is so strong? I have been the queen of the future living. I have had my life planned for that day's evening, tomorrow, next week, next month, next year, etc. I have had everything arranged besides that one tiny thing: the right now. Is that the reason I am overwhelmed and never have enough time? How do I stay in the present moment for a long period of time or even always? Well, the first mistake is I am picturing the future (again). *You can't stay present by picturing how you're going to do it in the future!* I am trying to see how my whole life will be in the present moment. Just the thought of it makes me exhausted and not wanting to make the shift to live in the present. Of course part of me is saying, "It is impossible. You might as well give it up now." But thankfully, my nagging voice is louder than the future part of me (the ego).

It is persistent, consistent, and keeps getting louder with each day. I just keep asking how. How? How? How? How? How do I stay in the present moment at all times with everyday responsibilities? Everything on my to do list has to be done.

For me it is my moment in the corner, when life keeps pushing and pushing to see how much I can take until one day I find I can't be pushed any more. I call it my corner trap. As long as I have even the slightest room to move, I will keep moving backwards, holding on to whatever it is I am trying to hold on to at the time, which in this case is the future. The instant I find myself in the corner and have no more room to move back is the split second I have to make a choice. I have two options: keep holding on, or let go (surrender). Clearly holding on has work for me (if it did, I would not be in my corner trap). So do I really have two choices, or do I only have one? I do have two. If I keep holding on, my consequences will be depression, anxiety, and breakdown. Like I said before, I am not strong enough to go through that. The only other choice for me is letting go (surrender). *As long as we hold on to being right, we create our own prison. By having the courage to be wrong, we let go, and that is how we get to freedom!* Both choices are very difficult. How do I let go when all my life I was trained to hold on and push through, be perfect and live for the future *(being right)*? I have had to realize by surrendering the future *(being wrong)*, I am gaining all the time I need right now. That one second, that split moment where I can't take it anymore—it is just plain all too much is also the flash of clarity where I can see how the present moment gives me all the time I need. It no longer matters whether I have five things to do that day or thirty-five as long as I stay present for each task and surrender the rest. Somehow it has its way of working out, and I am able to accomplish more that day than I have ever have any day living in the future.

I no longer rush through lunch with my children or anything else, thinking about the million things I still have to do that day, knowing there isn't enough time for me to do them, getting up from the table early to go be somewhere else. I am practicing presence. It doesn't matter if I am folding laundry, doing dishes, or having the time of my life with my babies. I am starting to always pay attention of how present I am for any given moment.

That moment in the corner trap when I want to scream and be angry because I am overwhelmed, scared, lost, and exhausted is also my grateful one because it provides an opportunity for me to have *a beautiful choice.*

Until now, I only knew how to act out of fear of what the future is going to bring, leaving screaming and yelling as the only option (I have done that plenty of times), which creates more pain. *Fear of the future brings out our insecurities in the present, creating pain. That leaves yelling and screaming as the only option in order for our body to protect itself!* Because when I am done letting out all my fear, I feel disconnected from my babies, and guilty about being a bad mother which is the most painful feeling for me. It is also a vicious cycle for me. Having the awareness that there is another option like choosing the now (which is love) and surrendering everything else brings forth a whole new me. It is hard to go from the old to the new, but given that I have spend more time in the corner than anywhere else, I am getting a good practice, in addition to feeling so good about every decision or action that is coming out of the present.

With every day it is getting easier and easier. I also take every situation as an opportunity to practice. Some are easier than others. For example, swimming with the kids in the backyard, playing games, watching movies, etc., makes it easier to be in the present moment. I love quality time—outdoors and nature. So the hot sun, perfect-temperature water and happy children are the easiest ways to practice living in the moment. I don't think about anything else like bills, cooking, cleaning, medicine, etc. I am just being grateful for spending quality time with Matthew and Jojo. Conditions like these make it possible for me to stay in the present moment for longer and practice. If I have learned anything, it is that if I am starting a new habit, it is OK to go the easier route. In this case, it is choosing pleasant situations to learn how to be in the now. *It is ok to choose an enjoyable moment when we are making the shift to live in the now!* I am looking for more enjoyable situations where I can practice, but it doesn't feel like another chore I have to do. That's one thing I cannot handle, another responsibility on my shoulders.

That has helped me change the way I look at things. Instead of living in the present moment being another thing to do, I look at it as a reward. In other words, I am reversing the process by changing my state, *a beautiful choice.* Instead of trying to do it all and be perfect for the days to come and postpone living in the present moment, I postponed all the future moments (even if it is responsibilities for that afternoon) and plans for days to come, to be imperfect in the present moment. *Postpone being perfect with living in the future and embrace being imperfect while enjoying living in the now!*

I no longer care if the house is spotless, if I am the perfect chef in the kitchen or perfect mother and wife always put together and having it altogether. I am just the best I can be in this instant. It creates a happy environment for my family, along with changing the balance of living life with cancer. The first few weeks everything I did or thought was cancer. Whether it was dealing with cancer, curing cancer, researching cancer, emotionally supporting cancer, or adding cancer to our life, it was just cancer, cancer, cancer, cancer. The balance was 99 percent cancer to 1 percent life. Being in the present moment is changing the balance to 90 percent life and 10 percent cancer. Why? I focus on being grateful for any given time we have to spend together trying to create fun memories. I am not sure what the future is going to bring, but I know for certain I want to live life fully.

As the weeks are going by and it is easier for me to live in the present moment on the ordinary day, I am starting to apply it to not-so-pleasant situations like doctor's visits, hospital stays, chemo treatments, and side effects. Those are still there and have to be done. I am thinking to myself, How do I stay in the present moment when my child is being poked by needles, filled with medicine that totally changes who he is, and being attached to devices that constantly make sounds that scare the —— out of me? *Gratitude* is the first answer that is coming to me. I am looking for ways and things to be grateful for. Anything and everything from the research being where it is with cure rates, to the dedication of the doctors, nurses, and any other medical or child life professionals that dedicate their lives to make each moment possible, successful, and pleasant. By focusing on their hard work so I can have it as easy as possible given the situation, I am able to look at any procedure or treatment as a blessing and a gift. Thanks to all the needles, medicine, and loud devices, Matt is able to live and do everything that he wants to. Yes, there are some limitations, plus a couple of hours or sometimes a couple of days where he doesn't have 100 percent energy or is able to do what he wants, but overall, he hasn't stop being Matthew.

If it wouldn't be for needles, yucky chemo, loud devices, and all the people working hard, there would be no Matthew at all today. *Practicing gratitude, even in unimaginable circumstances, is a key to living in the present!* Being grateful as well as present in hard situations also eliminates pain and helps me stay in the now to the best of my ability at a time. It definitely doesn't look the same way as in pleasant situations. However, my baby is with me and that is the most important thing for me. By being present in every moment and for every experience, we are able to grow from it, not just survive it. No matter how the experience goes, we are one step closer to knowing what works and doesn't work for us and how each of us reacts to different situations as well as what we need to change. Some moments are easier than others, but the hardest ones always have the biggest impact.

Like today it is Friday, our usual checkup day. I am thinking it's going to be easy. Just draw blood, see the counts, and go home (at least for me) and forgetting about Matthew—that to him it might not feel that way or that he doesn't really know what is coming, or doesn't trust what is coming. Maybe he just has had enough from all the past procedures that even blood draw is huge for him. We are talking about what today's visit will possibly be like. That we are just going to go in, draw some blood, see the count (by this time, even though he is only five, he speaks doctor's language) and go home. He is asking questions, like, "Do we get the big bandage today, Mommy?" Now to translate, to him that means "Are we going to the hospital?" and "Do we get to stay long, or do we get lots of medicine?" I have learned to listen and listen between the lines, which is another gift of living in the present moment. There is a lot of silence in the now, which is allowing me to quiet down all the unnecessary noise, opening my eyes, ears, and mind, in addition to paying attention. *We have to practice courage to silence ourselves in the now so we can hear the answer for the future! It is only by making the right choice in the present without thinking how it will look in the future do we get the results we want! Concentrate on what works for now!* It is scary to hear and be aware of everything. I am asking for it but getting it is terrifying because it makes the whole thing real and I am not sure if I know how to deal with it.

Deep down I know I have what it takes, yet the ego keeps creeping in trying to convince me otherwise. The ego is saying, "Sure, you have what it takes now, but what are you going to do later?" *Beware, the ego will do anything to put us in the future, create fear, doubt, and judgment; therefore, ego survives on scarcity! Letting the thoughts pass without reacting to them is the only way to stay present!* Reacting to ego thoughts is also why we get ourselves so busy in life. It is so we can't hear, see, or feel the now (the fear of it), which somehow give us permission not to deal with life. We do it by getting so busy doing other things, which gives us an excuse why we can't be in the now dealing with what is happening now. On the other hand, letting go of the future can be so hard because we can picture it the way we want it to be in order to protect ourselves. We can picture the future like make-believe; we can imagine it the way we want it or can handle it. Once again, it is the ego creating fearful thoughts of the now by making the future more enticing. In that it makes us feel we are not enough right now to handle the present situation, which would mean we will never be enough, and that is exactly what the ego needs in order to survive. I am telling you that ego will do anything to survive.

Presence is real, raw, and sometimes very scary, especially at first. We can't pretend cancer, pain, our or our kid's emotions are not real. We have to acknowledge it and, at the same time, deal with it, whether we know how right now or not. *Right now we have to do and be our best, which is imperfect, and that is why the ego is trying to convince us we can't make the right (perfect) decision for the future, making us doubt everything, especially our instinct, which knows we do have everything we need right now to make the right decision in the present that will create the outcome we want in the future!*

I am recognizing how it might look like it's easier to live in the future, but in the long run, it is really hard. It's like a merry-go-round, of fear and unwanted results, that never stops. That is what life in the future is. *The only way we can get out of fear and the future (merry-go-round) is by having the courage to change the present!* Dealing with each challenge as it comes, making mistakes or not, brings peace and unlimited abundance into our lives. So scary or not, there is nothing else that matters more than what my babies are saying or feeling right now. Acknowledgment alone is good enough. When my babies feel I am doing my best, it doesn't matter to them how good I handle things. My effort alone provides enough validation and shows them that being imperfect still makes them lovable.

So, I am thinking I am doing a good job explaining, educating, and getting Matt ready. Little do I know, I am wrong. On this particular day, Jojo is coming with us (winter break). The minute we get to the hospital, Matthew is heading straight for the doctor's toy room, Jojo follows, and they are having so much fun. I am thinking, *Thank you for the good day.* We are getting called to come in the doctor's office, and in an instant, things change. I feel it I am just not ready for it. I thought we were ready, and confirmed, but we aren't. The way Matt is walking, or I should say running in, I know he is scared, and it isn't going to be an easy day. Every time he runs and say "Mommy, you can't catch me," that means "I am scared. I don't want the needle, and I will do anything to try to make it not happen."

I am feeling thorn inside. On one side, I have Matthew who is scared of what is coming; on the other side Jojo (his sister) who is also scared of what they are going to do to her brother that he is so terrified. Then there is me being scared as a parent looking at my babies in so much pain, asking the question, how do I handle this situation in the present so we not only survive the day but learn and grow from this experience? I already know that no matter what I try to do, I can't take the pain away. How do I stay in the present moment now?

First, I am panicking and just for one minute, I want to run away and scream, "How am I supposed to handle this? What am I supposed to say? I can't do this anymore!" After that passes I get a hold of myself and change the conversation I have with myself. It is more like, "OK, take a deep breath. Take your ego out of this situation. It's not about you. It's about your babies. Think clearly. At least as clearly as you can and stay present."

I am playing catch with Matthew, having fun doing it and I do it like we have nothing else to do (not thinking about what is coming). I ask Jojo if she would like to wait in the doctor's room. After catching Matthew, I am trying to explain to him again why are we doing this and that we have to. It isn't going so well, however, we have gotten through taking blood pressure, temperature, and scale, but no matter how much I am trying to explain and make him feel at ease, I am not successful today. He is hitting, screaming, and biting. Jojo is in the dayroom, so she is not in the room for the needle. She is already traumatized from the walk in. She doesn't need to see more. Then at last the needle, take blood and done. So I think.

The nurse is putting the needle in, tries to flush, and nothing. I just want to scream, "SERIOUSLY?" (It isn't the nurse's fault.) This is also the reason Matthew sometimes doesn't trust that it might be "easy" visit, because every preparation for a visit comes with the final sentence, "If everything goes as we hope." She is trying to move the needle, and nothing. So finally, she has to pull the needle out and we will have to get accessed again. Now, that is something we are definitely not ready for. I know I am being tested on my skills of how to live in the now. Somehow this situation makes it easy. Being terrified of how we will get through the needle again, when he could hardly do it the first time, is putting me in the now like nothing else. Taking it one step at a time, focusing on each step, is making the fear go away. By eliminating all assumptions of how the next step is going to go or how this experience is going to affect his future, I am able to be 100 percent present. Love and compassion is filling my heart and I can feel how that is bringing some peace to Matthew. We are talking some more, holding on to each other to feel safer and are able to go through the procedure again.

We are all done, I am just sitting there asking myself, "What just happened? Did I do the right thing? Did I say the right thing? How is he really feeling right now? What about Jojo?" I am definitely in the present moment. That's the only thing I can handle (and I can hardly handle that), which makes everything so blurry. Being in the now means surrendering the past as well, even if the past happened just a few seconds or minutes ago, which makes it harder sometimes to remember things. Adding a traumatizing experience doesn't help the memory either.

I am feeling so exhausted. I just want to curl up in a ball in the corner and cry. But the visit is not over yet. We have to wait for the counts and the doctor hasn't even come in. Quickly, think, OK, I got it. I need a little time for me to gather myself and gain some energy, which is another part of practicing living in the moment, learning to enjoy time for myself without feeling guilty I should be doing something else or I should be stronger not to need it in the first place. I am telling the kids, "Mommy is going to make a cup of coffee while you are coloring with Ms. Kate [the art therapist], OK?" Thank you for the child life program and their support.

I am sipping the cup of coffee in total presence. That's all I have in me. I can't think of what I'm going to say or do when I get back to the room or how to get through the rest of the day. All I can do is drink the deliciously tasting coffee and just be.

After a couple of minutes, I get it somewhat together and catch myself heading back to the room to finish the rest of the visit. Thankfully, after all that, everything is going smoothly. I am getting the instruction of what to do until our next visit, when to come back, and we are good to go. But what now? The kids are in so much pain. I am in so much pain. And we are lashing out at each other. I feel myself leaving the now, which ultimately leads to a breakdown in the hospital hallway (right by the front entrance too).

"That is enough. Mommy can't take it anymore. We all need to use our words and talk about what is bothering us, but I can't take this screaming, hitting, biting, and anger," I say. There is a moment of awkward silence following the *What now?* question in my head. I know they are not really doing anything wrong; none of us just know at this point how to deal with all the painful feelings. At the same time, I can feel we are getting closer to knowing how.

I am looking at the kids and hear myself saying, "Today is a really bad day." My voice has the "I am overwhelmed" tone in it, which is surprising to me, because I don't know how to be vulnerable or show that I am falling apart. I know how to suck it up and be strong, but I just can't do it at this moment. I am begging them to talk to me, telling them I understand their pain since I am feeling it too. I just don't know, as they don't, what to do with it. This is a moment of *a beautiful choice* for me. Because in this instant (for the first time), I don't care about people's judgment or the future. All I am focusing on is Now, which is allowing me to be vulnerable, along with imperfect, giving rise to the better part of me, creating connection between me and my babies like never before.

It feels like we are in a bubble. It is just the three of us and nobody else. Nothing else matters. The only thing important enough is for us to hold on to each other even if we are struggling with knowing how. The only wrong way of handling this moment would be pretending it's not happening, brushing it off, hoping it will work itself out later.

At this point, none of us are really ready to talk about the pain we are feeling or don't know how, in addition to not having the words to fully describe it. So we start walking toward the elevator very quietly to have lunch in our special secret restaurant (tenth floor cafeteria) with views of the world. Yes, it is easier to be in the present moment when I am swimming or laughing with my children, enjoying my cup of coffee, but it is even more important to be in the now in the hard times. *Being in the now in hard times allows us to teach and guide our children through life experiences, providing them with necessary information to joyful, fulfilled life!* Those are the times that kids need us the most. They are also the times we grow the most.

After a long silence and surrendering the situation, halfway through lunch, we are able to talk about our pain instead of being angry with each other. Matthew is telling me that he was afraid of the needle because it hurts him too much. I am able to explain again that the cream he doesn't like to put on, because of the way it feels, helps make the needle less painful. He says he will try to put the cream on again next week and see how it feels and if it helps with the pain. Jojo is saying how scared and helpless she felt, not liking what they were doing to Matthew. I am admitting my fears and frustrations too about not being able to help more. We all feel relief. Our bond is stronger now. We know we are not perfect. We might not be able to change things, but we are always there for each other. Most importantly, we love each other with all our imperfections. In the present moment instead of numbing it and pushing it away planning to deal with it in the future. We are learning how to deal with our feelings.

That moment in the hallway has been life changing for me, kind of like giving birth to my children. I have been waiting for this trice (being present while truly surrendering the future) for a very long time with excitement, yet feeling scared that I might not be able to do it well. When it happened, the sense of unlimited, endless freedom—filled with love, connection, and kindness—felt like holding my baby for the first time. The world was perfect. Love was the only feeling, and every moment was filled with boundless courage to conquer the world. *In the present moment, we find all the courage to conquer the world!* For me, the difference between cancer and childbirth is in the opportunity of a second chance.

What do I mean by that? After my babies were born, I was filled with courage to change our world for the better, but as the weeks, months, even years went by, my courage went down with it. I settled for so many decisions and postponed many changes due to fear, making excuses that I will do it when the time is better. With cancer, there is no guarantee of a second chance. It is now or never.

The hallway moment gave me the everlasting courage to take actions all the time without letting fear in, making me doubt my decisions. From that point on, I have made a choice to always show up in life and take actions without waiting for a better time. It has been one of the best decisions I have made. Not because everything has been going smoothly and perfectly or we haven't had challenges thrown our direction but because no matter what is going on in the now, I always have the courage to be fully present the best I know how, living each moment like it is the last, eliminating any possible regrets of doing it differently in the future.

SUMMARY

- Treat each moment like it is your last.
- When you start learning how to be fully present, start with enjoyable situations.
- Reverse the balance of future and present moment.
- Trust that by being present, you will gain more than enough time to do what you need in the future.
- Know that the now will bring out the better part of you.
- The present moment allows you to be a listener and teacher.
- Practice courage to silence yourself to hear what you are searching for as well as the answers.
- Learn to listen between the lines.
- Accept being vulnerable and imperfect as part of daily life.
- Strive for creating fun memories.
- Learn how to be present for yourself.
- Practice gratitude and find things to be grateful for even in hard moments.
- Stop wishing for things or yourself to be different and have the courage to show up as you are at all times (imperfect).
- Embrace life no matter the circumstance.

Listening

What if all I have to do is watch and talk to my children?

I Am Loved!

Is written on the bear's sweater Matthew got from Santa this Christmas at the hospital. It is our first Christmas after he was diagnosed with cancer.

When I first noticed what it said, I felt concerned and even took it a bit personally. Why shouldn't he feel loved? Why shouldn't any child feel loved for that matter? Deep down I can feel a sense of profound message. My memory is taking me back to the time when I was working in the hospital and orphanage home during school years.

As a pediatric nurse, I was trained on children's psychology, compassion, and empathy. At school we did go over listening, but it was more leaned toward pain, symptoms, or patients' concerns as well as their comfort. I felt there is more to listening than that, especially with children. Working in the hospital I realized there wasn't ever any time left for anything extra. Getting through everything that had to be done medically for the children took all of our time. Hospitals were so understaffed. Everybody worked so hard to give the patients the help they needed, consequently not leaving any extra time for sitting down and listening to patients find words for what they were feeling.

Just to remind you, these were tiny little human beings just learning about life and feelings, so even if they felt something, putting it into words was a different challenge.

The orphanage home was a lot like the hospital. Even though there were no health problems (for the most part), there was so much to do to take care of all these babies, leaving only very little occasion for quality time.

I thought long and hard if I could spend the rest of my life being a nurse and focusing on the medicine side of children's health, but I knew I couldn't. I admire, along with being grateful for, every nurse and doctor that dedicates their lives to helping children get better. It just wasn't for me. I have always known in my heart that my work has been about connecting with children and figuring out how to help them cope with the stressful and scary side of being sick.

It wasn't until now (Matthew getting diagnosed with leukemia) that I can finally really crack the nut and dig in deep to actually see and understand the profound invisible source from which we could all gain the ability to change how we communicate, educate, and guide children (ourselves as well) through any sickness.

Matthew is asleep while I am sitting on the couch staring at the bear's sweater that says *I Am Loved!* All that comes to my mind is listening, because I feel that has a lot to do with the *"I Am Loved"* sign.

I have been feeling pretty good about my listening skills only discovering how much I really am not a good listener. Yes, sure, I listen to Matthew when something hurts, when he needs something, or when he clearly states what bothers him. But I have had absolutely no idea about the real struggles he has been going through or the real feelings he is experiencing since that is an undiscovered territory for me, as well as I can't even identify it within myself.

I know in order to help and guide Matthew with Jojo, I have to discover and learn how my body's feelings work in me. By watching myself and listening to my body, I have started to recognize the connection between every feeling and reaction. Every spoken word that has a different question and concern behind it. Every attempt to communicate and become aware of the contrary words to my feelings coming out.

Good listening is a key to feeling loved! When we listen, we validate the other person's feelings, which leads to feeling loved! Now the big question is, how do I become a truly good listener? What do I need to do to really listen? Is there more than one way to listen?

As days and weeks go by, answers are starting to come to me in an overwhelming speed and amount. There is so much to listening I am not sure if I will be able to ever get the hang of it. Anything I have learned until this point seems like a drop in the ocean. The last thing I want to do is to work on myself some more. How bad can I be? I have done so much work on myself. Is it ever going to stop? As much as I want to give up, feeling like I have done enough work on myself, I am an OK parent, or I don't have any more energy or time to give, life doesn't let me. I keep getting lessons thrown my way, whether I am ready to learn or not. I am starting to realize that it is more tiring and time consuming to ignore or avoid working on myself than it is to just do it. So from this point on, I will open myself, without resistance, to every opportunity coming my way to learn how to become the best listener I can be. *Trying to resist a lesson hoping it will go away is only going to bring a more painful one next time. It is more exhausting running away from change than it is to actually change!*

There are so many ways to listen, and it does seem very overpowering at first, but once you understand the basic, you can apply it to all areas of listening.

To be a good listener, we need to

- Ask questions, set our intention, and become aware of where our intention is coming from (place of love or fear).
- Silence ourself enough to hear the answer.
- Listen to what our child is saying, not what we are telling ourself or hoping to hear.
- Listen to our inner self and use it to guide us.

- Stop wanting to be right and try to see our children's point of view.
- Staying quiet is OK when our child's experience is different from ours and we don't understand.
- Repeat to each other what we have heard to avoid misunderstandings (we all process information differently).

What are all the ways we can listen?

- Listening for our and our babies' answers
- Listening to our and our babies' instinct (inner self)
- Listening to our and our babies' words and actions
- Listening to our bodies and feelings

It might look overpowering at first, but it all ties together, which makes it really easy at the end.

Listening for Answers

Asking questions is essential, otherwise, we have nothing to listen for. One of my first few questions when we confirmed it was cancer were, *How do we get through cancer and be better for it? How do we set our own expectations? How will I know what to do or guide each of us specifically to meet our individual needs as well as who we are?*

Listening to instinct has been the answer to my first question. By understanding love and fear, watching the way I feel and react to my feelings, along with the power of presence, I am able to live fully through each moment without leaving any room for regret or second chance to do things when I am more ready, better, stronger, etc.

The answer to the second question is to listen through words and actions, especially Matthew's. Since he is the one going through everything, he gets to decide how it is going to look and feel. We try to do everything we can to fulfill his wishes and help him make this challenge of a lifetime as easy as possible while trying to stay true to each of ourselves as well. He has wanted to stay happy, active and enjoy life like he did until cancer, so we strive for it in each moment.

The answer to the third question is the most complex, so it has taken every one of my listening skills to find the answer. I have learned that Matthew likes, besides the previously mentioned, to talk through his feelings. By staying active a lot and talking about what he needs, he has been able to cope with everything that is going on. Another way to manage his feelings is to cuddle, given his love language is touch. Jojo (his sister), on the other hand, goes into silence, because that is what she needs when she copes with a challenge. Her love language is quality time; therefore, I try my best to use any occasion for just the two of us to bond.

As you can imagine, it isn't easy since Matthew's cancer requires a lot of attention. On days I can't spend the time she needs with her, I at least try to acknowledge her feeling of disappointment about me not being able to give her what she needs. She understands it isn't because I don't love her, but me validating her feelings is very important.

When it comes to me, I am little bit all over the place. Laughing is my way of coping for sure, plus an active lifestyle (outdoors, sports) and silence. I take every chance I get to spend alone time in quietness, mostly nights or early mornings, since the days are busy and noisy.

This is one way of listening, and although they all tie together, there is a little bit of difference in each.

Listening to Our Instinct

Another way to listen is to pay attention to our instinct. ***Our instinct is the force behind every courageous thought or act! It shows us the way that is right for us, and all we have to do is be brave enough to listen.*** I could hear it from the beginning of our journey but haven't always had the courage to act on it. Thankfully, because of my wonderful children, I am able to find courage in situations I would not have before.

Like being happy, I have wanted to go through cancer that way but haven't had the guts until seeing Matthew doing it. That is giving me the push I need to stand up for what I believe in and follow the path that is made for us. Jojo is helping me on the path of compassion. She has shown me that compassion doesn't mean being perfect, it means listening, vulnerability, presence, and persistence. I have watched her try to be there for Matthew in a way you can only see in children. She doesn't always get it right, but through her unconditional love, she finds the courage to try over and over, no matter how hard it gets, till she succeeds. Watching her is giving me the courage to forgive myself for making mistakes, get rid of Mommy guilt, and helps me find the strength to try over and over till I get it right.

Listening through Words and Actions

The third possible way to listen is through the words that are coming out loud, whether it is while we are talking to a friend or family member. Whatever it is we are trying to solve will be the only thing we are talking about and can't solve in silence. Sometimes hearing our own words out loud provides the answer we couldn't hear in stillness. Talking out loud in front of our children while we are trying to solve a difficulty is very dangerous. For that children can't differentiate reality from our thoughts. They soak in everything we say as a fact and that is why I have been so terrified to project my fears on them through my words, especially because they were so little. *Children believe what we say (as parents) and act the way we expect them to.* Since my only personal memory about cancer was death, I have been afraid to speak, because I don't want Matthew to misunderstand and feel like the only option when you have cancer is dying. That is also why I have never talked in front of him about my fears (side effects of medicine, outcome, etc.) at doctor's visits, because I have known he would live up to doctor's knowledge as well. There have been many times where I have been feeling so frustrated and helpless and wanted to say more, but at the same time feeling like if I start talking, I will do more harm than staying silent.

I can't always explain it in words, but I do go with my instinct, trusting I will figure it out eventually and so far, I always have.

Listening to Our Bodies and Feelings

The last, but not the least, is listening to our bodies. In situations like ours, our children going through life-threatening illness, pain is a common denominator. Pain is one of the most misunderstood feelings. **When we don't hear our pain or the pain of our children, it leaves us or our children feeling abandoned, unsafe, and alone!** The reason it has been so hugely misunderstood is that we have never been taught how to correctly recognize or cope with it. *Pain, when we see it on the outside, looks like disrespectful, annoying, irritable, and uncontrollable behavior!* That makes us feel angry at the person as well as frustrated, furious, and livid, but what we really feel is being helpless, brokenhearted, and overwhelmed. Deep down we recognize our inability to help ourselves and our child, which is also our greatest fear.

On the other hand, if we learn how to listen between the lines (passed the behavior), we gain the power of *a beautiful choice* to react to the pain and not the symptom of it (the misbehaving). By separating ourselves from ego, we are able to guide ourselves and our children through the pain, validating that it is OK to feel that way.

For our family, pain shows up by being annoyed or snappy with another person. If the pain is big (which is not unusual given our circumstances), it comes out in a form of anger.

To give you an example, lately Matthew is being mad at me and pushing me away, not wanting to be hugged or me anywhere near him. It alarms me, given his love language is touch. I have been asking him why? All he keeps saying is that he feels angry all the time and can't stop but doesn't want to feel that way. I listen each time and for a couple of weeks, have been watching him. I am trying to figure out what the pain has been about as well as how to talk to him about it.

Going through cancer means going through so many different pains. I have tried many different ways to figure out how to help him with this pain but, so far, haven't been successful. Until today, that is.

We are playing Lego and I just keep asking. Finally, Matthew finds the courage to tell me he doesn't want to be hugged. "It doesn't feel good," he says. His senses change a lot with treatment, so I am not surprised.

Knowing about ego is helping me not to take it personally. "Thank you for telling me," I say. "Let me know when you are ready for hugs again, please?"

He looks at me with disbelief in his face and wonder in his eyes. "Why are you not getting mad, Mommy?" He assumes if he tells me how he feels, it will hurt my feelings (children do it a lot; even with the medical professionals, they are afraid to hurt others' feelings). *Assumption is the biggest obstacle in listening! When we assume, we abolish any possibility to communicate, therefore listen!*

"I don't want to hug you, baby, if it doesn't feel good. You should be very proud of yourself for finding the courage to let me know. Mommy is very proud of you." *It is so important to encourage our children all the time to express their true feelings and talk to us about their worries!*

Instantly I can feel a burst of energy filling up his body, a smile appearing on his face and joy spreading throughout the room. I am still not sure what this pain is about. Whether it is physical (sensitive pain to touch from medicine) or emotional (being afraid to speak up about his physical pain) pain. Maybe a little bit of both. However, I have no doubt that me listening for his pain instead of punishing the symptom of it validates his feelings. As a result, he feels safe, connected, and loved.

If I were to punish him based on the symptoms of pain (acting out, snappy), he would feel alone, unsafe, and unloved. That is why the teddy bear shirt says I Am Loved!

Everybody (parents, children and family members) feel the pain, medical professionals know about the pain, but nobody really talks about it. They might acknowledge the presence of it, but pain is like the big elephant in the room. Everyone knows it is there, yet no one wants to be the first one to say anything, especially when symptoms start coming out. Because who wants to tell a parent of a child with life-threatening illness "your child is rude or annoying"? Thus, each person waits till they absolutely have to or are asked for help. Even then they either politely say "I understand" or try to discipline the child to relieve the parents' pain, not understanding they unintentionally cause more pain.

For me as parent, I don't want to be patronized or protected. I want to know how to help and guide my child, not how to avoid judgment or uncomfortable situations.

I have appreciated everybody's effort to try to make it easier for our family. It is a very awkward position to be in on both sides in an instance like this. Yet I am not striving for easy. I want profound explanation.

I have taken my time to learn how to listen beyond the outward behavior. It has been the greatest and most proud accomplishment of my life. It not only confirms everything I have known till this point, it puts the word *unconditional* in unconditional love. It makes me more compassionate with myself and others and provides me with the answer I have long been searching for. I am a better parent, and it proves my belief that there is more to our bad choices than just intelligence.

Pain makes us more compassionate, open-minded, and connected if we choose to. It shows up the same in all of us. *When we learn how to recognize and cope with our pain as parents, it will help us create connection with our child like never before! For that reason, listening is the most important influence in parenting a child through life-threatening illness!*

Last but not the least fact I would like to mention about listening is this: *When we are ready to listen, we have to be ready to receive at the same time, because listening without receiving is worthless! We might hear the answer to our question, but if we can't receive it, we won't take actions; therefore, we won't get the results we want!*

What do I mean by that? Pain has been our constant companion on our journey, which has given me enough practice to recognize the many different ways pain presents itself. Where I have made the most mistakes, especially at the beginning, have been the times I haven't been able to receive the answer. There have been many instances where I could feel the pain in my children's behavior or mine only to doubt myself who am I to know (not receiving).

I was raised to believe that a bad choice is a matter of intelligence, not feelings. So when all of a sudden I am hearing the pain behind the choice, there have been moments where I could not have received the fact I know something more than what I was taught. I wouldn't listen to my instinct, because I wasn't ready to receive the greatness it had to offer. It created more painful consequences, which pushed me to learn how to receive by switching my old belief that greatness equals arrogance. By doing that, I have been able to take actions based on what I hear and not worry about others' judgment or mine about believing that bad choice comes from how we feel, not how intelligent we are.

From that point on, whenever I feel unease or irritation when we are going through scary or painful times, my radar goes on, and I listen for pain. I make sure we resolve the pain through talking and compassion instead of punishing the behavior. I surrender judgments, opinions, and convincement of others that I should tackle the behavior based on intelligence and stick with my guts. *We need to listen for our child's pain so we can help guide him or her through it instead of punishing the behavior and causing more pain!*

I am a better person for it and so are my children. Pain is still part of our life today and always will be. The difference is that we know how to recognize it in each of us. We know how to cope with it, therefore eliminating disrespectful behavior as a result of unrecognized pain—at least for the most part. After all, we are imperfect human beings.

SUMMARY

- Learning how to listen is an essential part of this journey.
- Start by asking questions.
- Practice courage and get quiet so you can hear the answer.
- Listening provides validation, safety, and love.
- Not listening equals feeling unsafe, alone, and not loved.
- Learn how to listen for pain—yours, your children's, and those of people around you—to eliminate bringing more pain into your life.
- Listening to your instinct is the greatest gift you can give yourself.
- Learning how to receive good things that come to your life is crucial to good listening.
- Without receiving, you can't take actions, resulting in producing more pain.

- Use everything you know about ego to not take what you hear personally.
- Feeling sorry for yourself will come, and it's OK for a little while, but staying in that state for a long time will bring more pain than validation.
- Talking, along with explaining consequences, will bring more positive results than punishing the behavior. Be patient. It will take time.
- Learn to listen to others' point of view. They have good intentions, just not enough knowledge, and even though it might not always come out right, they are vital for you to learn about the process of going through pain.
- It takes courage to listen to your instinct instead of judgment, opinion, or convincing of your ego, in addition to people around you.
- Stay strong, and always go with your instinct before your knowledge.

Doctors and Nurses

Do I set the expectations for them too high or too low?

Do I know what I really want and need from them?

Do I know the line that is not OK to cross, or do they?

Which side should say, "Hey, we are going to have a long-term relationship. These are the things I need from you"?

What are my boundaries, and how do I communicate it?

My answers to all these questions are "No" or "I don't know." It's not like it was part of my education growing up. So hearing the oncologist say, "We have the results from the test. Your son has acute lymphoblastic leukemia," besides "hmmm", a question-mark stare, and a "What do you mean" I am not able to come up with anything else, let alone think about the long-lasting relationship that is automatically forming with the diagnosis.

Hearing the doctor say those words out loud, which must have taken enormous courage for them to deliver, is definitely a moment I will never forget. For a brief second, everything I have known or believed is gone. Everyone and everything went blank. I think it happens for a reason. The pain of the news is so unbearable that the body goes numb. *Shock gives us a glimpse that takes us beyond the measurable offering and provides much-needed hope with guidance.* For me, it quickly confirms that from this moment on, I am starting life from scratch.

Almost everything I have known, believed, or hoped for is erased in a split second. What I thought was working isn't. What I thought I knew is gone. And I have nothing. The only option is to dig deep within to find the necessary tools to go on. I need to rediscover myself. And it all began the first night in the emergency room.

We are in the emergency room. Hours are passing by and finally, we are getting some answers—not the ones we are hoping for, but at least we are getting somewhere. Words like *infection, transfusion, getting admitted,* etc., are being said, yet at this point are not making any sense to me. Then there is the one word no parent ever wants to hear.

I keep asking for the doctor to give me some answer that would make sense to me. She has been trying to delay the possible answer as long as she can. But I am persistent, so finally, she says, "I can't tell you for sure, because we don't have the bone-marrow test to confirm it, but all the symptoms are pointing to leukemia."

Right after I have a public breakdown in the hallway and burst into uncontrollable tears while feeling like dying, I am running to the bathroom. Without me knowing, the doctor is following me. I am standing in the bathroom, leaning against the wall, with the ER doctor holding me by my shoulders. She is trying to stop me from falling to the ground, I think. She keeps on saying, "Listen, listen, look at me." I can feel how much she cares and wants to help me. She is trying to snap me out of the shock and make sure I am OK. She wants to catch my attention enough to make sure I hear the message she is trying to give me correctly. The message goes beyond the words that are coming out loud. It is the first experience that is giving me the gift of *a beautiful choice,* by opening my eyes to a new fact. *No matter what the conditions are in our life, the power is in the way we look, feel, or think about our circumstances! Life doesn't have to be what our assumptions make it out to be!*

Her actual words are, "If you wish your son to have anything, you want it to be leukemia. The research is so advanced, and the cure rate is high." See, my ego wants to attack her and fight, saying, "What are you talking about? Do you hear yourself? I don't want my son to have anything. I wish for us to go home healthy." But I feel the profound message she is trying to communicate to me from the higher powers, or the higher powers are communicating through her. She is trying to comfort me in the most painful time of my life, but instead, she is giving me the gift of a lifetime: the power of choice.

The fact that I can understand where she is coming from is thanks to the years I worked in the hospital. In situations like this, it sucks to be on either side. The instant of delivering the news takes a lot more courage. After all, you are changing someone else's life forever through bad news. It is something I don't think I was capable of or had enough courage for, and that is also why I decided not to pursue my carrier in medicine. I will always admire the healthcare professionals' courage to do their job as well as be thankful for it. Despite the unpleasant news they have to deliver most days, they get up each morning and dedicate their days to save the lives of our children.

When it comes to making a choice about my outward reaction, it is no brainer. I can attack the doctor based on my fears from previous experiences with cancer (everybody dying) or listen. I am choosing to find the courage necessary to listen—to trust my feelings that I can handle whatever news the message will bring and that everything is going to be OK, at least for now. I am taking advantage of the moment where everything is blank. I am letting the stillness provide me with the courage to embrace the part of me I have never even tapped into until this moment. It's a part based on feelings instead of knowledge, but it feels so right. It is proving to me how our bodies are incredibly intelligent and how we have everything we need within. All we have to do is listen and follow the guidance. *When our body goes into shock (denial), what it really does is creates a moment of stillness to let us see and feel beyond the measurable truth! It helps us open our minds to other possibilities!*

So after I process the message I return to the room and we are getting admitted to the hospital. Matthew needs two transfusions as soon as possible—something that absolutely terrifies me. I am so scared that the blood is contaminated with deadly disease. After just learning he most likely has leukemia, I don't know if I can handle more challenges the night might bring, except I don't have a choice. He needs healthy blood to get through the night. At this point, I don't know which news is more terrifying.

We are transferring to the second floor of the hospital, the children's oncology. The night is busy and filled with life-changing challenges. Matthew is getting his first transfusion. As the blood is dripping down to the tube and I watch it enter his body, I pray. I pray for the blood to be healthy, for the blood to help him survive the night and give him enough strength for us to figure out how to help him further.

A couple of days have passed by, and today is the day we will have the results of the bone-marrow test. I am watching the sun come up as I am sitting on the couch sipping my morning cup of coffee. Matthew is still sleeping. All I can do is just sit still without a thought. The numbness from the shock, along with the fear of what I will find out, keeps me in total stillness. I feel a sense of freedom. I feel no worries, no expectations, no pressure of outcome. Nothing. Just a place of total surrender. For a little while longer, I am enjoying this new state of existence.

My freedom is getting interrupted when I see the oncologist walking through the door. In a split second, I can feel the energy shifting in the room, and tension is taking over. My newfound freedom is gone, and I am back to reality. I am looking at his face, hoping till the last possible second that he will say Matthew is healthy, that all this has been just a misunderstanding. He starts talking to me, and with each word he is saying, my hope gets lesser and lesser till I hear the final word in the sentence—leukemia. There is no coming back now. I have no idea what he is saying. All I feel while staring at the oncologist is the formation of our relationship. At the same time, the answers to all my questions are taking place through my actions despite my readiness or ability to be aware of them. I can feel how my consciousness is working harder than my brain.

My fear of talking and saying detrimental information brought me a doctor of few words. He says only what needs to be said, allowing me to cope with the information in silence, just like I need, while patiently waiting for questions I might have.

I am realizing that whether I am ready or not, have the courage or not, these relationships between me, the doctors, and other healthcare professionals, are forming. I either allow myself to be a backseat driver and let the relationship just happen or take charge of the steering wheel and have a say in it. Either way, we are going to be in a relationship for a long time.

We also have another doctor who is more talkative. If I need to talk more, somehow the universe makes sure it is his day to visit with us.

We start to set boundaries through actions, which works for us, but I am learning that occasionally I need to use my words to clarify new boundaries based on our needs at the time.

It is not a comfortable factor for me. I was taught not to question the doctor and just listen. It was always kind of a one-sided relationship growing up. Telling the doctors now what we need has been a practice of courage, for sure. Nevertheless, it is easier to speak up for us than to pay the consequences of staying quiet. After all doctors are only humans too.

Not assuming that doctors and nurses know what we need at all times has assisted me in finding the courage to give them the information they need so they can help us based on our concerns without unnecessary frustration on either side. After all, their intentions are to make our journey as easy as possible. So me withholding useful information is only hurting everybody.

I am learning to shift the way I think. To go from "They know what we need and how we communicate. It is their job after all. That is what they do every day" to "I need to teach them how we communicate, what we need, and how we would like to be treated." It could not have been harder if I tried. I am realizing, like everything else, it has to come from within me.

The only problem is that I have no idea what my expectations are. What do I need? What do I say, or how do I set boundaries for myself? I have struggled to set boundaries or talk about my expectations in all my other relationships. How do I do it here? This relationship is one of the most important ones. My son's life is in their hands.

I ask, and I sure receive. I know I have to do the work on me first. I have to figure out what I want and need first so I can recognize it in Matthew. *We have to get to know ourselves first. Learn what our needs and expectations are for the relationship first! It is then we can teach the doctors or other medical professionals!*

I have had to understand the influences and heal in order to learn how to set healthy boundaries. I have taken advantage of the mirror effect. Every time someone is doing something that bothers me or I don't like, I ask myself questions. Why does it bother me? How would I do it differently? Is it something I would like to improve? The answer is always yes. The key to making the shift and change things is within me.

The minute I have the courage to admit it is my struggle and ask for guidance how to make the change, I gain the power over my life instead of giving it to someone else. *It is in the courage to admit our struggles we gain the power of a beautiful choice to live our life instead of giving the control to someone else!*

It has felt selfish at first, yet at the same time very empowering. I have been taking baby steps and practice courage every day to be me and stand up for me. For the first time ever, I am experiencing what it feels like to be in charge of my life. I am letting go of my security blanket of blaming someone else for my struggles, and as scary as it is at times, it is pushing me to get out of my comfort zone all the time, face my fears and work on growing myself. It is giving me the greatest reward of being and standing up for myself. Now I can teach the same to my kids.

How is it helping me in the relationship with doctors and nurses? Knowing myself and what I want while separating myself from ego (telling me I am not enough) has opened my eyes to see an important fact. *Doctors are humans too and want to be validated as much as we do! They might not know what to say or do at times just like us! It is with this understanding we can form a relationship on the foundation of love and filled with compassion for another human being! In that everybody feels validated; therefore, we get the results we want!*

I have used the mirror effect as guidance. It has been helping me to recognize when I am not being impeccable with myself. If they don't live up to my expectations or I feel irritated with the fact they should be doing more, it shows me I am being too hard on myself, setting up unrealistic expectations.

Learning to be compassionate with myself instead of achieving improbable goals is hard for me. I have been associating my thoughts of Matthew's survival with achievements of doctors and nurses, as well as mine. I am only glad I have figured out it is not true. *Cancer isn't about doing! It is about us being and knowing that we are enough right now! We don't have to do anything to prove that, just be!*

Making this shift in my thinking process is life changing. I am learning how to just be. When I am in the state of being, I am at peace. I have sensible expectations, which releases a lot of pressure from myself and doctors. I am aware of what we need and want from the doctors as well as nurses, and I am able to recognize how fear influences our anticipation.

What I want is certainty and guarantee. I am recognizing more and more that is something I will never get on this journey. I can also see now it is the hardest part of the relationship between patient and doctor. My fear wants to hear the doctor guarantee Matthew's survival, and when they don't, it leads to irritation and, ultimately, anger. I want to blame them for not trying harder, not knowing more, but deep down I know they are working harder than ever. I know they want nothing more than to be able to guarantee me my baby's life. That is why they chose their jobs in the first place. They have dedicated twenty to thirty years of their life to learning how to save my baby, so I can only imagine how hard it is for them, working endlessly yet not being able to provide certainty. That is true dedication. *Doctors show up every day so our children can have a chance at life! They are giving us certainty and guarantee by showing us they will always stand by our side while we are facing the challenge of our lifetime! Let's not miss this fact anymore! It is in knowing that we find peace, surrender the outcome, and find the courage for a true second chance at life!*

It is a journey of surrendering control over life and recognizing what is behind the wants and needs. It is about letting go of the assumption that certainty, along with guarantee, will bring joy, peace, as well as happiness into our life. It does, we just have misunderstood the definition of *certainty*. Fear makes us believe that by having assurance of the future, we can have everything else. Consequently, we want guarantees from the doctors because they are the ones having the ability to cure our babies, which brings joy, peace, and happiness into our lives in the future.

Finding joy, peace, and happiness is in understanding that we are enough now and we have the certainty of this moment. By changing our expectations of the future and focusing on the present, we find true freedom. Love, laughs, and enjoyment of each moment is something we all strive for our whole life. We can have it all in the now. We just have to learn how to find it through love (inner part of us) instead of trying to control it by fear (trying to control outside circumstances).

That eliminates the pressure from the doctors to do magic and helps us set healthy boundaries for our relationship. By letting go of certainty of the future, we gain the power and control over our lives now. No longer do we need to control the outcome by holding the doctors or anybody else responsible. We no longer need precise circumstances or outcome to feel in control of our life. We know we are in control of the present moment, and that is the power of *a beautiful choice.*

I am the first one to let the doctors and nurses know as well as ask about what needs to be done in order for each of us to be able to do our job effectively with enjoyment while making Matthew and Jojo feel safe. It brings respect into the relationship, painting a clear line for both sides of what is OK.

I am grateful for all healthcare professionals that dedicate their lives to our sadness, and I appreciate their work, which is sometimes so painful and unrewarding. Nonetheless, they show up each day doing their best no matter how hard it gets or what outcome they get. Their determination is my true inspiration!

SUMMARY

- Define expectations for yourself first before you anticipate them from doctors and nurses.
- Understand that cancer (or other illnesses) is about being, not doing.
- Know that you strive for joy, peace, and happiness through certainty of the future, but you can only find it in the present.
- Recognize how fear wants guarantee from doctors, which they can't give you, creating frustration and anger.
- Learn to surrender control over future life.
- Invite joy, peace, and happiness into your life now, letting go of dependence on precise circumstances or outcomes.
- Embrace the power and control over your life that comes from the courage to admit your struggles.
- Be grateful for the dedication of all the healthcare professionals.
- Recognize how they are standing by you in the most challenging times of your lives like no one else.
- Be inspired by the doctors' and nurses' true dedication and determination.

Siblings

How do I guide Jojo without scaring her more than she already is, honor her feelings, as well as make her feel part of the journey?

As I am lying peacefully next to Matthew after he has fallen asleep, my thoughts keep slipping to Jojo. How is she feeling right now? What is she thinking about? Is she OK? My heart is broken into a million pieces. Our whole life just fell apart and I am realizing there will be more moments in her life I will miss than the ones I will be part of. I am not sure if it is something I can handle. Since the day she was born, I have been there—every day, every moment, every first, every experience. The separation right now is unbearable. I have no idea what the next couple of days is going to bring, but right now, I don't think I can handle it.

I am trying to dig deep within while crying quietly for help. It is a sleepless night. As I am sitting on the couch watching the flashing lights go by, my life is flashing in front of me. I am trying to find answers there somewhere, asking myself all kinds of questions. Did life get me ready for this experience? Has there been a point in my life where I missed this important lesson? Do I or will I know how to guide Jojo through this painful journey? Her three-and-a-half-year-old brother just got diagnosed with leukemia. She has no idea what cancer is, and I was hoping she wouldn't have to know till later in her life. Now not only will she hear the word *cancer*, she is going to know it in association to her brother. How do I introduce the word *cancer* to her without putting my feelings of fear behind it? How do I guide her through this experience of a lifetime if I don't even know how to go through it myself? What do I say?

My Mother Bear is coming out of me right away. I am going into protective mode, which I feel isn't the best thing, but I am doing the best I know how now. I can't feel guilty or bad about it. *Feeling guilty only puts us in a self-punishment frame of mind and consequently, we take actions that are even more detrimental!* Our thinking process focuses on punishing ourselves for not being a good-enough mom! That closes any open doors for an opportunity to learn or grow and we just end up hurting the sibling more! *It shuts love with compassion completely out, leaving ego in charge of everything, producing unwanted results by creating vicious, self-punishing, cycle!* The ego strives, but the relationship with the child (sibling) goes down the drain.

Like everything else, I am realizing, in order to guide my princess through cancer successfully I have to do the work on myself. Learning about my feelings, how I deal with scary situations, and knowing my role helps me recognize that it is what Jojo needs too. Protecting her is actually harmful and making her feel left out. Am I protecting her feelings or mine? Do I trust myself that I can handle everything, that I am strong enough? Not at this point. I feel fragile, vulnerable, scared, and overwhelmed. The little girl inside me is crying for help because she has no idea how to handle all the feelings that are running through her body or how to process all the information. I keep sitting on the couch trying to figure out how to guide Jojo.

The biggest misunderstanding about siblings feeling left out is that they are jealous! Yes, there is little bit of that too, but the majority of them feeling left out is about fear. By me protecting Jojo and trying to keep her away from scary information or situations, I have been participating in her assumptions about everything that is going on. Since she only has very limited facts about what is going on with her brother, her imagination goes wild. That creates untrue beliefs and does more damage.

We are all scared and don't know how to cope with fear at this time. Even without words, sometimes the energy of fear kick-starts a domino effect of assumptions. There are moments where Jojo feels like, "It must be really bad with my brother, and he is going to die since no one wants to say anything in detail." It is not that we don't want to say more; it's that we don't know as much as she doesn't. We want certainty as much as she does, but by trying to protect her instead of being vulnerable with her, we bring about the feeling of her not being enough for us to share with her the experience. That results in making her feel left out.

She wants to be part of everything as much as we do. She wants to help her brother and have a role in the family. My fear of her losing her innocence as a child is harming her more than any scary information. *Protecting a sibling from scary information only results in a feeling of abandonment, loneliness, and overwhelming fear!*

It is the toughest time in parenting for me. What I thought was good seems to be bad, and what I thought was bad seems to be good. I have to start redefining my parenting values and strategies.

It has taken me months to figure out how to guide my baby girl through her brother's cancer. It hasn't been till I have discovered how my feelings work beyond the obvious and became compassionate with my own feelings, guiding myself instead of protecting myself, that I have been able to do the same for Jojo. By feeling my pain and recognizing I am OK if I do, I have learned how to go through sorrow, as opposed to running away from it while discovering it is a lot easier to face any terrifying experience than paying the long-lasting consequences of numbing. I am able to guide my baby girl instead of protecting her by working together with her on figuring out how she can help (what her role is). How much does she want to know? How does she want to be communicated with? How does she recognize fear as well as cope with it, and what makes her feel left out and why, and how can we change it? *Working with siblings on their expectations is a key in order for them to feel safe and loved!*

It has provided the necessary outlook for me as well as broke the pattern of assuming kids can't handle pain. She hasn't been as afraid of pain as she has been afraid of not being there for everybody. She wants to be able to do something as a sibling as much as we want to do as parents. *Siblings strive for being able to do something to help as much as we do as parents!*

I have learned and truly believe that as a sibling, Jojo takes her brother's illness harder than a parent. It makes sense to me, because children have an unbelievable bond with each other that no parent can ever understand. Till this day when something is going on with my brother, whether hard times in life, unfair treatment or something else, I feel so caring and defensive in a way my parents can't. Knowing that and reminiscing my feelings for my brother makes it easier to understand what Jojo goes through.

Every time I feel lost, I picture that particular situation with me and my brother trying to see how it would make me feel. *We need to put ourselves into the shoes of our child by feeling how we would feel if it were our sibling!* That always brings compassion and love into being, giving us the tools to think from a place of love instead of fear. We are able to relate and understand how the sibling feels.

By understanding how I've felt is how she feels, I am able to explain to her that we all feel like we have no decisions when it comes to trying to control cancer. We can control this moment and how we choose to live it. We can have control over our reactions to our feelings. Painful and fearful emotions will automatically come, but if we recognize them we have the opportunity to either grow from them or numb them, consequently creating the future we either want or are afraid of.

Together we have been able to figure out her role as a sibling as well as clear out the misunderstanding about her trying to protect us as parents. ***Children have this unfortunate ability to blame themselves for their parents' mistakes as well as trying to fix them and make us parents feel better!*** When Jojo gets overwhelmed by the pressure of not being able to influence and fix outside circumstances (protect everybody's feeling and mistakes), her room gets really messy. When I try to talk to her, she denies anything is wrong, until she can't push her feelings down anymore and they explode. The explosion of her feelings matches the explosion in her room. It will take time to break the habit of holding her feelings inside trying to protect us parents. We all have to learn how to communicate about our feelings along with hers.

I always try to make sure I acknowledge her feelings about conditions being unfair and teach her from my mistakes instead of putting my mistakes on her. We keep learning to recognize our reactions to feelings in new situations. Most importantly, we focus on loving her the way she recognizes.

Like couples, children communicate with their parents through love language. There are five love languages:

- physical touch,
- words of affirmation,
- act of service,
- quality time,
- and receiving gifts.

Dr. Gary Chapman

Knowing everyone's love language eliminates lots of misunderstandings, frustrations, and hurt feelings! It helps avoid the feeling of being left out, in addition to not feeling loved. For me, knowing Jojo's love language is quality time is helping me in making sure I make effort in finding time to spend with her any way she wants. Ten minutes of quality time makes up for hours of attention that is given to Matthew. She understands he needs my time. What makes the difference is the thought and effort I put in creating the space for me and her. That is why ten minutes makes such a big difference.

Every day we work on our relationship. We expend it in places we were too afraid to even go into not too long ago. I am learning to admit my fears, imperfections, and mistakes to her, teaching her from them. No longer is there an unclear line between my life and hers. We do occasionally cross the line and project our feelings on one another. The difference now is that we can admit to it and grow stronger from it instead of growing bigger frustrations between us by blaming each other.

Jojo has never complained about not having enough attention. I make sure I recognize her for it on a regular basis. Her unconditional love, compassion, determination, and persistence is my inspiration for life. I am learning so much through her eyes and will forever be grateful for her presence in my life as well as an honored that she is my daughter.

SUMMARY

- Feeling guilty for making mistakes only causes more harm.
- Kids feel left out because we try to protect them, not because they are jealous.
- Siblings take the illness the hardest due to their extraordinary bond with each other.
- They need a role to feel part of the family and cancer journey.
- They need guidance through pain with explanation of consequences (hurting themselves more by acting on pain instead of going through it).
- They need to be treated as equals, because they are.
- They go through the same feelings, so by learning how yours work, you are able to teach your child.
- Learn from them. Their unconditional love, compassion, and determination is inspiring.
- Know their love language.

Family and Friends

Do I know how to be a wife, daughter, sister, or friend?

It is a quiet, dark night at home. The kids are sleeping, and I am enjoying the breeze coming through from the open windows with the sounds of nature. While I am sitting alone, I wish my family could be here with me. On the other hand, the thought terrifies me. I am so broken, confused, and lost right now about life. I am trying to figure out where I went wrong. What actions or decisions in my life have led to this moment? Why did I move thousands of miles away from my family? How is my marriage over? We haven't said the word, but I know it is over. In one split second, life crashed right in front of my eyes, and I have no idea how to fit in. I have no idea how to be someone's daughter, sister, wife, mother, or friend. I have absolutely no idea. With the moment where everything went blank, hearing the diagnosis, life has started over. With that, so did all my relationships with family and friends. I just don't know how to be in any relationship right now. I don't even know how to be in a relationship with myself.

I am starting to rebuild my life and rediscover myself in a new light, which is something I have not expected to do in my thirties. I thought I would have all my relationships figured out by now. In a way, I do. I know how not to be someone's someone. I feel the first step is to forgive myself for not being a good daughter, wife, sister, mother, or friend. I know right now it is very hard for me to put any attempt in any relationship because I can't even do it for myself. I am working on forgiving myself for excluding myself from the world and everyone. I am not sure if it's the right thing to do, but that is all I can do right now. I feel like my actions have caused so much pain to my family especially, and I am afraid to do or say anything right now. Plus I feel the only things I want to say are hurtful because I feel scared, which triggers angry feelings, and all I want is for someone to take all my pain away. Mostly my parents or my husband. When they don't, I can only feel my frustrations building up, and more confusion is entering my space. I keep wondering, *why don't they love me enough to save me? Help me? Show me that I am worth trying? Are they just showing me, mirroring back to me, how I feel about myself?* I feel the answer is yes. With all the pain that is going on all around me, I can't stand to cause people even more pain. So for now I am allowing myself to separate from everyone while I try to figure things out.

My requirements from friends are low, but my anticipation for my family is high. Given I have high expectations from myself, it does make sense. I can relate to friends about how awkward it must be when your friend's child gets diagnosed with a life-threatening illness. As for my family, I am realizing my expectations are high because I want them to save me and take away the pain because I don't believe I have what it takes to save myself.

My ego wants my parents to do my job. I have been assuming they are supposed to protect me the same way I have assumed I am supposed to protect my babies. I am so afraid of everything that is going on in my life, which only makes me angry with my family for not making it better. ***When we don't trust ourselves that we have what it takes to save ourselves, we get angry with people around us for not taking our pain away!***

Learning how fear works is helping me to let go of the assumption and anger. My fear of how I am going to go through cancer, help my babies, and be able to handle all that, creates a vicious cycle of blame in the hope of trying to save Matthew's life. I believe, or maybe more hope, that if I throw my worries on someone else (my family), the worry won't exist; therefore, cancer won't exist, and Matthew can't die. ***Fear always gives power to outside sources, leaving us with inside frustrations!***

Pain is the cause of me being angry with my family. I don't want to feel any pain and therefore I blame them for bringing me on this earth or not being there for me. For not being able to take my pain away. What it really is about is my frustration and anger about not being able to take the pain away from my babies. *Everything we struggle with the most we mirror on people close to us! In this particular situation, we project our inability to protect our babies, which isn't our job to begin with, on our parents by blaming them for not being able to protect us! We only get back more pain as well as do to our kids what we complain about our parents doing to us!*

By understanding my job as a parent, I am capable of letting fear go. Recognizing I am supposed to guide my children through their lessons in life with unconditional love and surrendering my assumption of protecting them from life (controlling how their life turns out to be), I am able to truly forgive myself for all the pain I have caused myself and my family. I am opening my heart to love, creating a safe environment for everybody around me.

I am learning how to communicate with my parents and set new boundaries for our relationship. I am able to accept a very important stage in parenting. *We all do our best as parents, and sometimes our best isn't good enough, and that is OK as long as we can admit to it!* With that, I am releasing the guilt that all parents carry around about doing more, and I am not defending my parenting skills.

By living in the present moment my heart is opening up to unconditional love of just being, watching, and guiding my children as my parental duty. Surrendering my assumptions about protecting my babies, or my parents needing to protect me, is allowing me to learn from them as much as they learn from me. For the first time, I can call that a relationship since it's founded on the participation of both sides. We help each other grow as human beings instead of one side telling the other how to live or be. In this space, there is no room for fear of judgment, disapproval, disappointment, or feeling I should be or do more. We all feel we are enough with all our imperfections.

I am trying to apply these principles to my falling-apart marriage. I am succeeding in a way, I know I am. It just isn't presented to me in the way I pictured it. I am a more compassionate human; I just don't have enough to give right now to be a good wife or partner. Even though we are in the process of a divorce, I feel a new, more profound relationship forming. It is a relationship founded on love. We might have lost the marriage description to our relationship, but we have found and have been strengthening our bond as humans, friends, and family. *We do have to "lose to win" to get what we want! Our focus is on recognizing that we are getting what we ask for!* I have lost my title as a wife, along with the traditional definition of what a thriving family should look like. What I am gaining is everything I have always strived for: a family where we all love and respect each other while growing as individuals in pursuit of our dreams and life's purpose, along with the solid foundation of support and strength to withstand the storm of all the challenges to get us there. Me and my now-newfound friend (soon to be ex-husband) may not have the traditional romantic love, but we have human love for each other, and that has been something worth working towards.

I am opening my ears to listen so I can provide the much-needed validation for myself and everyone around me. It is allowing me to see things in a whole new light, generating healthy relationships with family and friends. Everything the fear projects on my family with friends, mostly in silence, has something to do with my doubt— doubt that I have to do better, be better, take bigger actions, or know all the answers; otherwise, I am a bad parent and friend. All these assumptions are going away by me accepting myself with all my imperfections. Everything is starting to make sense by me understanding love and fear thoughts as well as trusting myself that I am good enough and have what it takes within. *In the instance we trust we are enough and have what it takes within, we start to project love, compassion, and joy, getting back the same! By trusting ourselves, we obtain the necessary peace we need for our journey!*

Giving up trying to be someone better is bringing me the biggest peace. I show up as I am at any given moment, imperfect. It is hard but I know it will get easier with each courageous act of being myself, no matter how big or little. I am making sure I keep refreshing my intentions to stay true to myself every day. I see what a difference it is making in all my relationships. They are growing into more loving, giving, and meaningful.

Being grateful for each moment with opportunity to learn more about a person provides a safe platform for mistakes and misunderstandings, strengthening bond with each individual, including ourselves, through compassion! We are able to disagree while listening to each other's points of view without judgment or taking things personally!

Every time I chose to act from a place of love, I chose *a beautiful choice*, and I am able to say how I need to be treated or communicated to avoid hurt feelings.

Also, vulnerability establishes a secure place for expressing all emotions and allows me to teach people about what is OK and what is not.

It is crucial to teach people around us, with compassion, what our boundaries are! For me, there are certain things people can't say. When they do, I feel my blood pressure rising, and anger starts to take over. That is my clue to teach them what they said is not OK to say. It isn't always comfortable because they have good intentions, but I have to stay true to myself.

My biggest button pushers are: "He is going to be OK," "If this were to happen to anyone," "You are so strong you handle it well," "You have to be positive or you have to . . ." Basically, anytime they are trying to guarantee an outcome they can't influence or try to tell me what I have to do, I shut down. I hate to be patronized or lied to. What people that are not in the situation don't understand is they haven't earned the right to say certain things and never will. It's not personal, they just have to learn to respect parents facing such challenges, but we have to learn to respect ourselves first. *We need to teach people around us that there are certain things they haven't earned the right to say! It is our job to teach them, with compassion, what they are!*

All people around us have to do is just show up. Whether they know what to say or how to solve a problem doesn't matter. For me, when I see their imperfection, their vulnerability, it offers me more comfort than anything else. It gives me the confidence that it is OK not to know. It is more important to show up. I am learning so much through my family and friends and growing into a better parent and strongly believe they are an important piece of the puzzle on this journey. Not an easy one, but significant.

Setting our own expectations about family and friends is utmost important! I remember meeting a family on our Make-a-Wish trip, and I will never forget the moment we talked about the role family and friends play in cancer. The mom was so passionately describing her experience, only I was listening with dumbfounded feeling of sorrow and confusion. She was proudly telling me how her family and friends did exactly what a particular person (I don't remember who that person was precisely) said they would do. Stuff like not understanding, not living up to whatever she needed, not being supportive and just being judgmental know-it-alls. It was so distraught to me it left me speechless. I couldn't think about anything else that night, wondering why is such an assumption out there for the world to believe?

It has taken me awhile but I have figured it out. All this misunderstanding is created by fear. The fact that we were raised to give our power to outside sources to control our happiness. The minute we give power over our life to someone else, hoping that person will save us, no one can live up to any of our expectations or be compassionate enough. *When we leave our pain in someone else's hands, it only destroys the relationship!*

Giving our power away works for a little while. People feel sorry for us, and it feels good and right for the time being. Then they try to help, which makes us mad. Next they give us space to figure things out for ourselves, which makes us furious. Last they give up. Why? No matter how much they try to be there for us, *if healing doesn't come from within ourselves, we will attack people, making them feel less than and never good enough! We push them away through disapproval of ourselves!*

Fear makes us feel like we are not able to find acceptance, joy, peace, and happiness within ourselves, like we can only get it through someone else. That is the ego. It is also the root problem in any relationship. *Our misunderstanding that we can't make ourselves happy, that only another person can do that for us, creates frustrations in any relationship, ultimately pushing the other person away!* If we can get past our ego, we discover our true self and our power within to be brilliant. We are able to get past our fears and break free from all misunderstandings in a relationship. Because all insecurities are ego, which strives for certainty and wants to be right in order to feel validated. We are afraid if we are not right, we are not enough, which eventually pushes people away from us. *We assume if we can be right, we can get the outcome we want, not recognizing that by being right, we are acting out of fear, getting the results we are afraid of!*

I am thankful for every encounter coming my way and teaching me as well as providing answers for me I am striving for. I know that no matter what challenge we face in a relationship, life, or parenting, everything we need has been with us all along. All we have to do is go beyond ego and discover the untapped world of unlimited potential within us.

SUMMARY

- Recognize that you try to put your fears and pains on people close to you.
- Use the mirror effect to help you cope and find what you are looking for.
- Don't assume you have to do or know more in order to be a good parent, friend, daughter, wife, or sister. Showing up just the way you are at any given moment is more than good enough.
- Being vulnerable and imperfect makes you more compassionate and understanding.
- Learn to respect your emotions, and you will be able to do the same for family and friends.
- Learn to say what is OK and what is not with compassion; it only strengthens any relationship.
- Set your own expectations of how you want your relationships to be. Don't let other people tell you.
- Never assume people know what you need.
- Learn it is OK to ask questions about how the new relationship is going to look, what is OK to talk about, or what each of you needs.
- Both sides are learning new boundaries, so patience is essential.
- Everything you are looking for is already there. All you have to do is open your heart.

Education

**What if I could understand how feelings affect
my life? Would my life be different?**

According to Elizabeth Kübler Ross, there are five stages of grief:

- Denial
- Anger
- Bargain
- Depression
- Acceptance

I thought that grieving only comes after loss of someone. When I looked at the definition of *grief*, I was surprised, yet it made sense. It explained so many assumptions or misunderstandings. **Grief *is keen mental suffering or distress over affliction or loss.*** Affliction is the key word. All these emotional roller coasters, exhaustion, and anxiety finally have a name: *grief.*

When I heard the words come out loud from the doctor's mouth, "Your son has leukemia," I didn't realize that I am going to spend the next three years and four months grieving. First, I grieved the dream I had for our family, then the loss of the life as I knew it, then the loss of our son. He didn't die physically, but I knew cancer was forever going to change who he is. It didn't matter whether the changes were going to be good or bad, the fact is, he is going to go through the biggest challenge of his life, and that is going to change who he would have been without it. On top of that, there are all the everyday afflictions, like changes in treatment regiment, spinal taps, hospital stays, side effects, fear of getting sick with pneumonia, flu, etc. The fear of what the day is going to bring, am I going to make the right decisions, and I can go on and on.

Knowing the grieving process is very important. So we can respond to a fact of the given information, not the feeling we are going through. Why? If we know, for example, we are at the anger stage of grief when we are presented with unexpected, new, scary information, we can separate the anger from the fear of the given fact. *That split second provides us with the moment of recognition so we can react to the fact of the new information and not to the emotion of the grieving process, therefore producing the result we want.*

I am learning it the hard way. We just got admitted to the hospital for a high fever. Matt is so sick and in so much pain like never before. I am in so much pain watching him. Right now I am also going through the anger stage of my grief. I am so angry that life is not going "perfectly" as I have always pictured it would. Here I am, trying to guide Matt through one of the most painful happenings. I am so angry and frustrated. At some moments I'm thinking, *Why is this happening to him? Isn't cancer enough?* Instant like this, when the pain is unbearable, always bring me clarity. I know it, but right now I am not seeing it yet. I am recognizing the grieving anger (life not going the way I planned), and I am able to put it aside from this situation. Also, I am working on owning up the fact I am terrified. Acknowledging my feelings is still something I am working on. It has been getting better, but I am still not ready for critical situations like this. Ready or not, here we are.

I need a moment of silence to really allow my feelings to pass. Matthew's pain with his fever are so intense and continuous there hasn't been any time for peaceful silence, or is there and I am missing it? It has taken me a day, but I am figuring it out. In conditions like these, my moment of silence has to come in the midst of all the commotion and noise. Once again I can feel the beauty of our bodies and intelligence of it. Matthew has been in excruciating pain for twenty-four hours now. Watching him go through it has been harder than finding out he has cancer. My body is feeling so overwhelmed; thus, I can feel it slipping beyond the mind, thought, and ego into a space of silence for much needed clarity. It is happening at the same time as I am surrendering the need to be strong. On the outside, I am sitting on the bed across from Matthew crying, telling him how much I love him, how sorry I am, and how hopeless I feel that I can't take his pain away. This is the moment I have strived for. *This is the exact state that allows us to have a much needed moment of recognition from beyond the thought in order to feel the outcomes of each decision.*

I can feel if I act on fear, it will only bring unwanted outcome. The fear makes me yell at people around me, hoping to make Matthew's pain go away, but by doing that (that's what fear always does—attack), I will only create more pain and make Matthew feel alone as well as less than. On the other hand, choosing love makes me go through the pain and sadness feeling every bit of it allowing compassion and validation to grow. Even though it is not easy to sit by his side not being able to fix things, it does much more for both of us. It creates a space where we both feel loved and safe despite the pain. Me being vulnerable, crying and showing my hopelessness validates everything Matthew is feeling, therefore showing him it is OK to feel like that, validating him as human. *Validation is where love abides our being, creating an unyielding bond.* It has taken four days to get rid of the pain. We have kept hanging on to each other the whole time, which not only strengthened our relationship, it affirmed our belief that as long as we feel loved, we can get through anything.

Each stage of the grieving process happens for a reason. If you choose to see it, you can find what you are looking for and admire the intelligence of your bodies. Here are some of the ways I used each stage of grief to help me grow and find what I have been looking for.

Denial

I knew I had no idea how to parent and guide a child through cancer, help the sibling, or be a wife, daughter, and friend. Denial bought me the time I needed to find peace with my imperfections, my insecurities, and my not knowing how to handle scary, hard times by allowing myself to pretend cancer wasn't serious and life threatening. I strived for ordinary moments that didn't get affected by cancer or treatments. Where I could forget about cancer. Like swimming, swinging, reading books, enjoying home-cooked meals together, and kissing my babies. In that time (denial), I have been able to find the courage to acknowledge (to myself and my children), that I might not know how or what we are going to do to get through this, but I am here, ready to learn and be here for you guys the best I know how. Because it came from a loving place, I was able to be open-minded to hearing what they needed to say or how they felt. In a beautiful way, it made us closer, safer, and loved. Why? *Kids don't expect perfection or for us to know everything. They look to us for compassion and understanding that only comes from staying true to ourselves and admitting that we are not perfect, but we are here willing to make mistakes to figure out our new life.* We were working together every day trying to figure out each of our lives, feelings, how we deal with our feelings, and what we want. It took me eight months to go through this stage since I knew our lives are changing forever, not just the length of the treatment, so I allowed myself to have all the time I needed to get it right.

Anger

Ohhh, this one took the longest, two years. I wasn't angry twenty-four seven. Sometimes for a moment. Sometimes all day or a couple of days. Sometimes once a week. I just couldn't let go of the disappointment that life isn't how I envisioned it. I was trying to hold on to something that was already gone, which gave rise to frustration, leading to anger. I was already so tired from everything that was going on as well as the amount of fear I was feeling; the last thing I needed was anger. All I wanted is just to be and enjoy the time we all had together. During this stage I have learned about love and fear and discovered the misunderstandings in parenting about the state we operate out of. It wasn't until I was able to let go 100% of any certainty, old belief, and control that I found peace. Each day I got an opportunity to let go a little and understand more. It was up to me to practice courage of embracing the unknown. Understanding that what I thought was love when it came to parenting was really a fear gave me a sense of freedom and control. *Freedom, in a sense, is that we might not be able to control life, but we can control each moment we are given by choosing to make the best of it, no matter the circumstance.* Showing up all naked (that is how I felt) with all my insecurities and vulnerabilities to parent my children like I never did before, in the moment no longer waiting till I am better, stronger, more perfect, has given rise to an unforgettable feeling of love. With that, I have been able to move on.

Bargain

I became a great negotiator and doer with this stage. For the first time in my life, I have kept every promise and finished every task. My son's life was the greatest inspiration for practicing courage to take action and show up in life. Before cancer, I have lived my life in thoughts and dreams. I would occasionally take actions toward my dreams, but only within the safe comfort of the known. Deep down I was mad at myself for not having the courage to live and enjoy my life the way I wanted, furthermore creating the cycle of ongoing fear. I was feeling less than with each defeat which created a world filled with frustration, bitterness, unhappiness, and lack of excitement or joy in anything I did. I believed that by not taking certain action and listening to my fears, I was being a "good," responsible parent. Avoiding mistakes and failure is all I knew that defined a "good" parent. The Bargaining stage helped me see that *giving into fears and avoiding taking action does not teach love; therefore, we can't get the results we want. It is only when we practice courage to overcome fear, by taking actions, can we create a place filled with love, joy, happiness, and compassion.* From that point on, I have watched all of us grow into confident, loving beings embracing our authentic selves. For the first time in my life, I felt like a really good parent.

Depression

It showed me that *just being is always good enough*. I have always strived to know more, do more, achieve more, hoping one day I will be enough. I will be lovable and worthy for someone to stop and pay attention to me. I have spent thirty-five years going after more only to realize it will never be enough. *No matter how much more we do, be, or know, as long as "more" is attached as a condition, we will never reach the feeling of love and being enough.* Depression had minutes, hours, and sometimes even days filled by being. The exhaustion of the physical body and mind as a side effect of depression opened a new door for me. I was not able to do more, so I was forced to surrender and just be. When I allowed myself to go with the flow of depression and just be, I have never felt anything more refreshing. It was scary at first, but after a while, I loved the feeling of being and enjoying each moment without the guilty pressure of doing, knowing, and achieving more. After a couple of months, I felt comfortable enough to practice being without the help of depression. I made it part of each day to find a little time to just *be* and feel good about it.

Acceptance

It taught me to embrace life as it is at every moment and every situation. Accepting that whatever I am going through right now is a gift, not a disadvantage, helped me open my eyes to see the invisible, open my mind to feel the illogical, and open my heart to love the unlovable.

The grieving process has been a roller-coaster ride. Part of it has been; I haven't realized how often I have been going through one or that I have been going through multiple ones at the same time. I recognized it at the beginning, although I talked myself out of it. After all, I assumed you could only really go through the grieving process when you lose someone physically.

But when the grieving over the loss of Matt as I knew him kept showing up over and over I felt there is a bigger message behind it and I started to pay attention. I have spend hours watching him sleep trying to understand why I feel a sense of loss; after all, he is still here. Sticking with my hunch is paying off. Going through the different times in his treatment as well as recalling what I was feeling proving that even though I feel one way due to the grieving process, I have been able to respond to facts of the situation or information instead of the stage of the grieving process I am going through just by being aware of what is going on.

As mothers (I don't want to speak for fathers even though I think they feel the same), we live every day under this constant pressure of being strong and holding everything together. We think if we show our struggles or feelings, we won't be good parents or just plain old good enough. Vulnerability is not even an option. Adding grief to our insecurities of not being enough or not acknowledging our feelings is like skydiving without a parachute. No matter how strong and brave you are trying to stay, eventually you are going to crash with disastrous consequences following.

Understanding what our bodies are going through, along with being compassionate and gentle with ourselves, is one of the most important missions on this journey. It is what education is about. *If we understand the emotional effects, we gain the power to choose how we react to them. We get that moment of stillness, that split second, before we react and words start coming out. It's that split second that makes the world of difference not only in our life but in our children's as well.* In the quietness of the trice, we are able to realize how grief has an effect on our mind, our thinking process, along with our reaction, as well as getting to picture or feel how we would like to react, how we would like to live through this moment. *It is in those invisible moments we make the biggest differences.* That stillness provides the objective point of view of the situation. By understanding the grief and being able to separate from it, you are able to see things as facts instead of emotional assumptions. You can clearly identify your needs and the needs of your children. You are able to provide guidance through listening not only to yourselves but to your children as well.

Validation and the feeling of safety will be the result of decisions that come out from the stillness, which is a place of love and abundance instead of grief and pain. Answers will become available no matter the circumstance, empowering you with a sense of safety, accepting that unwanted or scary situations will keep showing up, but you can change how you experience them. Avoiding or hiding from them because you are in a grieving process will only result in more anxiety.

So how does one begin to recognize how grief influences responses? Thankfully, it is fairly simple. Hard, yet simple. *It is important to understand the stages of grief and to believe we have a choice.* In situations like this, where your child's life is in danger, there is the preconceived notion of not having a choice. Assumptions that fear along with grief is the only appropriate response is an expectation set out by years of previous responses that came out from not understanding human emotional being well enough to be able to practice courage of following the unexplainable feeling through our instinct. If it is not something that can be scientifically proven, then it is wrong. That is what we are taught to believe.

Working in a hospital for years, I have seen that over and over. I have always known there has to be a different way. I have spent the last twenty years searching for the answer. Slowly through opportunities, research, and instinct, I started to unravel the mystery, but it wasn't till I found myself in the hospital room with my son's life in danger where I really confirmed my answer. *Our emotional state of being is equal to, if not more important than, our physical being.* It's a complex system of unknown potential for most of us, which is why it is so hard for us to believe we have other options besides the known, fear, and grief. *As humans, we like certainty, so we stick with the known even if it doesn't work for us.* Following our instinct or knowing what to do in situations like this is considered absurd, arrogant, denial, or sometimes even plain old crazy and rude. Practicing courage to follow our heart isn't how most of us were raised. Believing we have everything we need inside us for any given scenario is something most of us never even thought to consider. So when you find yourself in the hospital surrounded by all educated people with scientific proof behind every piece of information they are throwing at you, how do you dare to believe in yourself and follow your instinct? How do you separate yourself from feelings and information influenced by others? *We need to learn to trust ourself by creating a quiet and still place where no judgment, opinion, or life-collected knowledge based on fear exists. It's in that place we find our true self.* The tranquility of that moment enables you to react to any given situation or challenge in loving response without the fear of preconceived notion. *In that stillness unearths guidance to any question we have.* That place provides appropriate response to any given struggle life brings our way, and that is what educating our children undergoing cancer treatment or any other serious illness is.

We, as parents, are here to guide our children and teach them about their feelings. Our job is to provide validation that everything they are feeling is normal and OK and that they have everything they need within them to make decisions that works best for their life and who they are. Or as Wayne Dyer said,

> **Parenting is not about having children lean on you, it's about making leaning unnecessary. They've got a compass. Let them follow their own compass.**
> **—Wayne Dyer**

The second part of education is about the physical body. It is very important to understand the emotional being, along with love and the reaction of fear, because you want to keep information just that, information. You want to leave your feelings out of the facts about the illness. Attaching our feelings creates preconceived notions for the child of how he or she should react or feel about what is going on in his or her body. I know this is where I have used the denial stage of grief to my advantage. I allowed myself to numb every feeling of fear I have had for the moment so I can provide facts for Matthew without really putting my emotions behind it. My intention has been to avoid him living up to my expectations.

What has helped me? I still haven't fully processed that cancer goes with Matthew. Once again that goes to prove that we have everything we need within. Our body goes through the grieving process without any of our conscious effort in order to protect itself and also provide necessary time and guidance for the next step. Denial has helped me and my babies protect our bodies from shutting down due to enormous amounts of pain and fear we have been experiencing. *All we have to do is listen, follow, and take advantage of the automatic response of our body that is so beautifully designed to protect itself without any of our conscious effort.* After all, it is there to serve us, not hurt us.

Allowing myself to embrace denial I remember telling Matthew he has leukemia, which is a cancer of white blood cells, as if I was telling him he has strep throat. I even explained it like that. After we watched the French animated movie for kids about how our bodies work, the episode about leukemia, I could explain to him why he has to take the medicine for so long to fix the bad guys (white cells) in a way he could understand by comparing it to strep throat bubble-gum medicine. Something he could picture and understand. He knew if his throat was hurting, he had to take bubble-gum medicine to make it better, and even though his throat stops hurting, he has to take the medicine for a few more days so the pain doesn't come back. The same goes for leukemia. Even though the bad guys (damaged white cells) go away after a short while, we have to take the medicine for a lot longer so they won't come back. This simple answer and video is providing enough information for him for the time being.

For older children, this would not be satisfying, but Matthew has no knowledge about cancer, so I want to keep it simple. I want him to understand how his body works, but leave an open room for his questions.

We consistently continue to educate ourselves and answer questions about what we need based on the reactions of the body or feelings at the time. I never ask what will happen or how his body might react, because I don't want his body to react subconsciously to the information he is hearing, which are only previous experiences of someone else. It has been allowing his body to react to any medicine in its own way, creating its own experience based on his body. I always assure him that it's OK, that his body is feeling whatever it is feeling after the medicine because even though the medicine is helping him get better and gets rid of the bad guys, sometimes it makes other parts of the body hurt, which shows me that our bodies know what is best for them.

Most of the time when Matthew has been hurting, he runs, swims, or dances. My fear wants to stop him, because I am afraid he is going to hurt himself, and that's not how cancer patient should act, but deep down, I know and feel I need to let him. Why? *Endorphins can act as nature's morphine, dulling pain. And the power of our minds helps us switch focus from the pain to something else, making the pain go away.* So if I allow him to be himself and run, swim, etc., I not only help him with his pain, I also empower him by teaching him that he knows what is best for his body. ***In that lies the power of* A Beautiful Choice, *teaching our children that they have everything they need within and at any time can use it to solve their situation while teaching us as parents who they are.***

Even though we have faced a few side effects along the way, I know we have avoided many more by not knowing about them. By learning how our bodies work emotionally and physically, we have been able to make our own path through cancer, along with teaching people around us how we like to do things and what works for us. Matthew has taught me it doesn't matter how big the body is, there is always an intelligent human being inside knowing, through instinct, everything they need to know to guide them.

SUMMARY

- Your fear of protecting your kids from bad things is your limitation. You are not able to protect them from life, but by educating yourselves and them about how your bodies work, you are able to teach them healthy responses to challenging conditions.
- If you believe they can, they are likely to believe the same.
- Set intention and allow your body to help you achieve them.
- Create a trice of tranquility; it will provide guidance and answers.
- Teach your kids about their instincts and the power within they have of knowing what is best for them.
- Focus on what they can do instead of what they can't.
- Let them speak about how their bodies feel after medicine instead of telling them in advance how their bodies should feel through information based on fear and other people's experiences.
- Assure them they won't hurt the doctor's feeling if they tell them how their body feels or what doesn't work for them.
- Teach yourself and them about their illness based on facts, not emotions.
- Know endorphins can act as nature's morphine, dulling pain.
- Teach yourself and your kids about the power of their mind to make the pain go away.
- Validate your and their feelings even if they scare you.
- Know sadness never feels safe; acknowledge it for yourself and your child.

A Beautiful Choice
Through Children's Eyes

THE MAGIC OF CANDY LAND

The whole concept of *A Beautiful Choice* originated from watching my kids while being reminded and inspired about the view of the world through children's eyes. They have the gift of the magical vision. Something we all used to have, but somewhere along the way to adulthood, we lost it. I would love for *A Beautiful Choice* to bring back magical vision to all of your eyes, to remind you that no matter what challenge, how strong the storm, or how unfortunate life may seem at any given moment, there is always a magical rainbow waiting to be seen by you. There is always sunshine waiting to bring you light into a dark moment. There is always the opportunity for you to put on your pink glasses and view the world the way you like it to be instead of how it is. Change always starts in our vision, seeds in our action, and sprouts in our love. *The power behind flourishing change that moves us towards a loving world is in practicing courage to dream! To dare to dream through children's eyes! To surrender our pains as security blankets and take a step forward into the world we once believed and now only wish for! This is the time to surrender false hope for a second chance and*

96

participate in creating a wonderful world with the chance we have now!
How we began?

It hasn't really been one particular event that opened my eyes. There have been lots of little moments. One kept coming back and it is on this experience we have built the rest of our world.

It all started when we were hospitalized for treatment. It was our second day in, out of the four-day treatment, a couple of weeks after the diagnosis, when we discovered the movie *Candy Land: The Great Lollipop Adventure.*

Like our dreams, I have found it hidden in the back of a drawer, almost forgotten. I almost didn't pick it up because I didn't identify it as something Matthew or I would like. Yet my instinct kept guiding my hand toward the corner to pick it up. Since I couldn't resist, I picked it up thinking we could always watch it for a couple of minutes, and if we didn't like it, I could return it.

In an instant we started to watch, Matthew loved the movie more than anything. From that moment on, he watched it over and over. Not only for the two days we stayed in for this treatment but also each time we would come to the hospital for treatment. It would be the first thing he would look for right after we checked into our four-star hotel (hospital room).

It gave him something to look forward to. Even on the days we had to get admitted unexpectedly due to need for blood transfusion, platelets transfusion, etc., we could switch our moods from disappointment to excitement by bringing up the movie.

Pretty soon even our world outside the hospital started to turn into Candy Land. Mostly in the car or sometimes on walks, we would pretend what the world would look like if it were made out of candy. We turned trees into licorice, houses into gingerbreads, clouds into marshmallows, flowers into lollipops, and on and on. I have enjoyed watching the kids make this make-believe land of sweetness. At the same time, there have been instances where I could see them sink into the world of their own, feeling the magic of a wonderful world according to their vision. World filled with love, laughter, joy, and fearless possibilities.

It has helped us change scary car rides to the hospital into enchanting experiences. Ordinary days have taken on delightful turns just by simply changing the way we look at each moment, each challenge, and each opportunity.

Our magical vision started the shift in our world, but it has been our actions, persistence, and determination that have kept it going. It has been our courage that has started to change the world around us and has turned our dreams into reality. It has been our surrender of certainty that has created the world of safety. And most importantly, it has been our courage to trust within ourselves that we have everything we need to make the shift. What started as a dream and magic is now our reality.

A Beautiful Choice has given us the power and encouragement to change our world, and we hope it will do the same for you.

To be continued.

COURAGE

C—**celebrate** every moment no matter how good or bad.

O—**open** our eyes and mind to unrecognized possibilities and dreams.

U—**uncover** true love and compassion even in the most painful times.

R—**recognize** the power we have to change our life and those around us.

A—**ability** to bring light even to the darkest moments.

G—**grateful** for each moment and blessing.

E—**enrich** our lives and those around us by love.

Edwards Brothers Malloy
Thorofare, NJ USA
June 1, 2016